CGP Practice Exam Paper
Edexcel International GCSE Biology

International GCSE Biology

Set A Paper 1

AF126794

| In addition to this paper you should have: |
| A ruler. |
| A calculator. |

Centre name				
Centre number				
Candidate number				

Surname	
Other names	
Candidate signature	

Time allowed:
- 2 hours

Instructions to candidates

- Write your name and other details in the spaces provided above.
- Use a pen with black ink.
- You are allowed to use a calculator.
- Answer **all** questions in the spaces provided.
  There might be more space than you need.
- Answer multiple choice questions by putting a cross in the correct box.
  If you need to change your answer, draw a horizontal line through the box.
  Then mark your new answer as normal.

Information for candidates

- The marks available are given in brackets
  at the end of each question.
- There are 110 marks available for this paper.

Advice to candidates

- Try to answer all the questions.
- Carefully read each question before you try to answer it.
- If you have time at the end of the exam, check your answers.

For examiner's use

Q	Attempt N°			Q	Attempt N°		
	1	2	3		1	2	3
1				7			
2				8			
3				9			
4				10			
5				11			
6				12			
Total							

Answer **all** questions in the spaces provided

1   Wing length in fruit flies is controlled by two alleles.

Vestigial (short) wings are caused by the allele '**n**'.
Normal length wings are caused by the allele '**N**'.

The vestigial wing allele is recessive to the normal wing allele.

(a) What does it mean if an allele is recessive?

☐ **A**   Two copies of the allele need to be present
            for the characteristic to be displayed.

☐ **B**   Only one copy of the allele needs to be present
            for the characteristic to be displayed.

☐ **C**   The allele only has a very small chance
            of being passed on to offspring.

☐ **D**   There has been a random change
            in the base sequence of the allele.

(1)

(b) Two fruit flies with normal length wings are crossed.

(i)   Complete the genetic diagram below to show this cross.

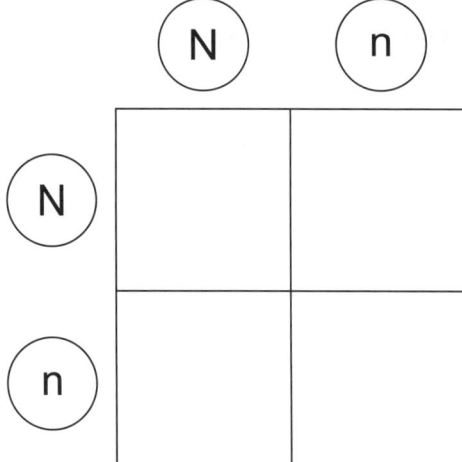

(1)

(ii) The two fruit flies crossed in the genetic diagram have 200 offspring. Calculate how many of the offspring would be expected to have vestigial wings.

Expected number of offspring with vestigial wings = ...

(2)

(c) Fruit flies are eukaryotic organisms.
Describe how the genetic material of a fruit fly is stored in its cells.

....

....

....

....

(3)

(Total for Question 1 = 7 marks)

2   Quadrats can be used to investigate the population sizes of organisms in a habitat. A group of students used 1 m^2 quadrats to investigate the plant species that live in a small strip of land next to their school.

They divided the land up into two sections, as shown below.

They placed three quadrats at random in each section of the land and counted the number of buttercups, clover and dandelions in each quadrat.
Their results are shown in this table.

| Plant | Number counted per m^2 | | | | | | | |
| | Section A | | | | Section B | | | |
	1	2	3	Mean	1	2	3	Mean
Buttercups	54	50	52	52	60	65	64	63
Clover	70	74	69	71	87	96	88	
Dandelions	3	5	4	4	13	12	11	12

(a)   Explain why the quadrats were placed randomly.

....

....

(1)

(b) (i)   What is the median number of buttercups per m^2 in section **A**?

median number of buttercups per m^2 in section **A** = ...

(1)

(ii) Calculate the mean number of clover per m² in section **B**.
Give your answer to 2 significant figures.

Mean number of clover per m² = ...
(2)

(iii) Section **B** measures 5 m by 3 m.
Use the data in the table to estimate the total population of dandelions in section **B**.

Estimated total population of dandelions in section **B** = ...
(2)

(c) Use the data in the table to give a conclusion that about the population sizes of the three plant species in sections **A** and **B**.

....

....
(1)

(d) Give **three** examples of abiotic factors that may affect the number of plants of each species growing at different locations on the land.

1. ....

2. ....

3. ....
(3)

(Total for Question 2 = 10 marks)

3   *Salmonella* is a type of bacteria which causes disease in humans.

(a) Which of the following infectious diseases can also be caused by bacteria?

☐ **A**   pneumonia

☐ **B**   malaria

☐ **C**   influenza

☐ **D**   AIDS

(1)

(b) The diagram below shows a *Salmonella* bacterium.

(i)   Give **two** features of the bacterium which show that *Salmonella* is a prokaryote and not a eukaryote.

1. ....

2. ....

(2)

(ii) *Salmonella* bacteria can enter a person's body via contaminated food. They cause illness when they reach the cells of the intestines.

Suggest **one** way that the human body is likely to defend itself against infection by *Salmonella* once the pathogen has been ingested.

....

....

....

....

(2)

(c) Viruses are another type of pathogen. Viruses are not cells, and are much smaller than bacteria.

(i) Give **two** structural features of a virus.

1. ....

2. ....

(2)

(ii) An example of a virus that infects plants is the tobacco mosaic virus. Describe the effect that this virus has on tobacco plants.

....

....

....

(2)

(Total for Question 3 = 9 marks)

4 In eukaryotic organisms cell division can take place by mitosis or by meiosis.

(a) The diagram below shows part of a eukaryotic organism's life cycle.

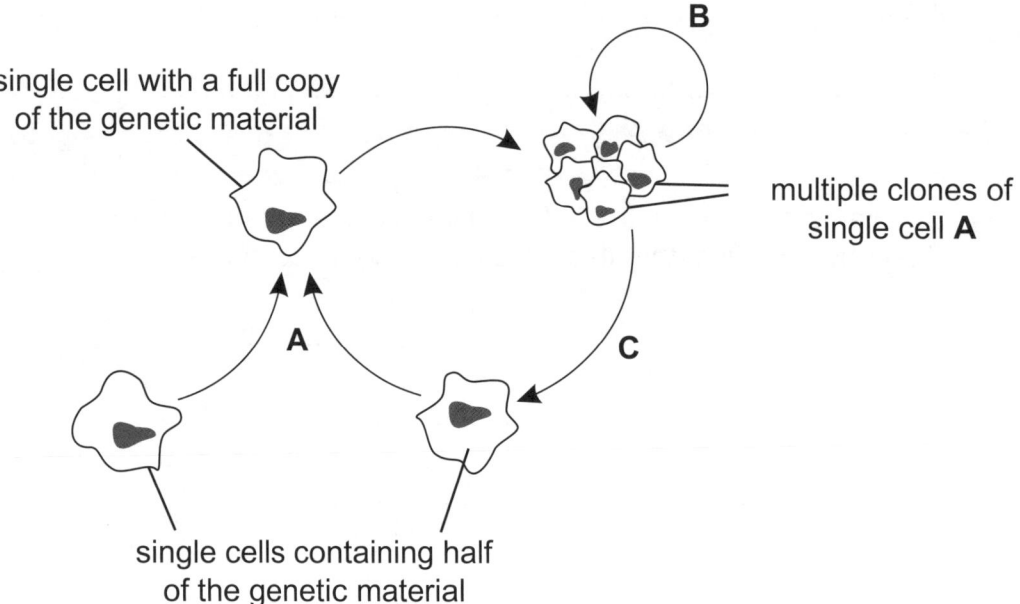

(i) Which of the stages, **A**, **B** or **C**, shown in the diagram involves mitosis? Give a reason for your answer.

Stage: ....

Reason: ....

....

....

(2)

(ii) Name **one** process in living organisms, other than reproduction, that involves cell division by mitosis.

....

(1)

(b) Which of the following sentences about cell division by meiosis is correct?

☐ **A** It produces two diploid cells.

☐ **B** It produces two haploid cells.

☐ **C** It produces four diploid cells.

☐ **D** It produces four haploid cells.

(1)

(Total for Question 4 = 4 marks)

5 Selective breeding can be used to produce organisms with useful characteristics.

(a) This photograph shows a Labradoodle. Labradoodles are dogs that have been bred from a Labrador retriever and a poodle.

A Labrador retriever's gentle temperament makes it popular as a guide dog for people with sight difficulties. However, Labrador retrievers shed a lot of hair, so they can be unsuitable for people with dog allergies.

Labradoodles were first created in order to provide guide dogs for people with dog allergies.

(i) Suggest **one** characteristic of poodles which first encouraged guide dog breeders to cross one with a Labrador retriever.

....

(1)

When a Labrador retriever is crossed with a poodle, the results are varied.

Some of the puppies do not have the right temperament for being a guide dog. Some of the puppies are not suitable for people with dog allergies.

(ii) Describe how Labradoodle guide dogs, which are suitable for people with dog allergies, could be consistently produced using selective breeding.

....

....

....

....

....

....

....

(3)

(b) A farmer has used selective breeding to increase the yield of her crops, and is now looking at other methods to increase crop yield.

(i) The farmer used to grow aubergines outdoors, but now grows them in a glasshouse. This resulted in a higher yield of aubergines.

How are the conditions in the glasshouse likely to have been different from outdoors, in order to give this result?

☐ **A** decreased carbon dioxide and decreased temperature

☐ **B** increased carbon dioxide and increased temperature

☐ **C** increased carbon dioxide and decreased temperature

☐ **D** decreased carbon dioxide and increased temperature

(1)

(ii) Another farmer wants to increase the yield of his farm's wheat crop. He applies a chemical to the wheat fields.

Suggest what type of chemical the farmer has applied, and how it could help to increase the wheat yield.

....

....

....

(2)

(Total for Question 5 = 7 marks)

6   The diagram shows a marine food web found near a deep sea vent.
A deep sea vent is a place where hot water issues from the ocean floor.

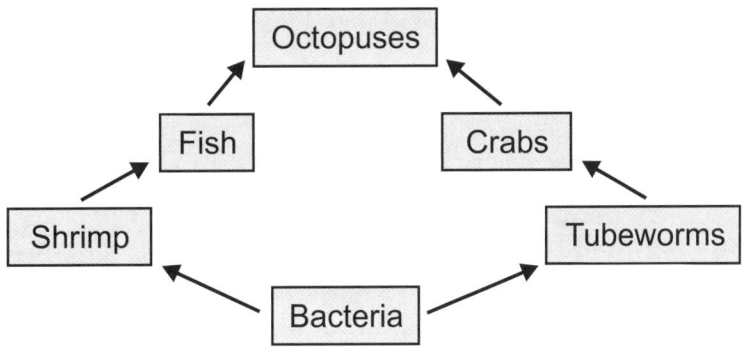

The producers in the food web are bacteria. They get the energy they need to increase their biomass from chemicals produced in the deep sea vent.

(a) Give **one** similarity and **one** difference between how these bacteria act as producers and how a typical plant acts as a producer.

....

....

....

(2)

(b) Which of the following is a secondary consumer in the food web above?

☐ **A**   Tubeworms

☐ **B**   Octopuses

☐ **C**   Shrimp

☐ **D**   Fish

(1)

(c) When the fish feed on the shrimp, only 10% of the energy available in the shrimp is transferred to the biomass of the fish.
Explain why most of the energy is not transferred to the biomass of the fish.

....

....

....

....

....

(3)

(d) Explain how a fall in the population of tubeworms could affect the population sizes of the other organisms.

....

....

....

....

....

....

....

....

(4)

(e) The diagram shows an incomplete pyramid of energy transfer for one of the food chains in the food web. Each bar is drawn to scale.

The bar for shrimp represents 12 000 kJ of energy.

Draw a bar on the pyramid to show 1200 kJ of energy at the fish trophic level.

Octopuses

Shrimp

(1)

(Total for Question 6 = 11 marks)

7 The diagram below shows a cross-section through a leaf.

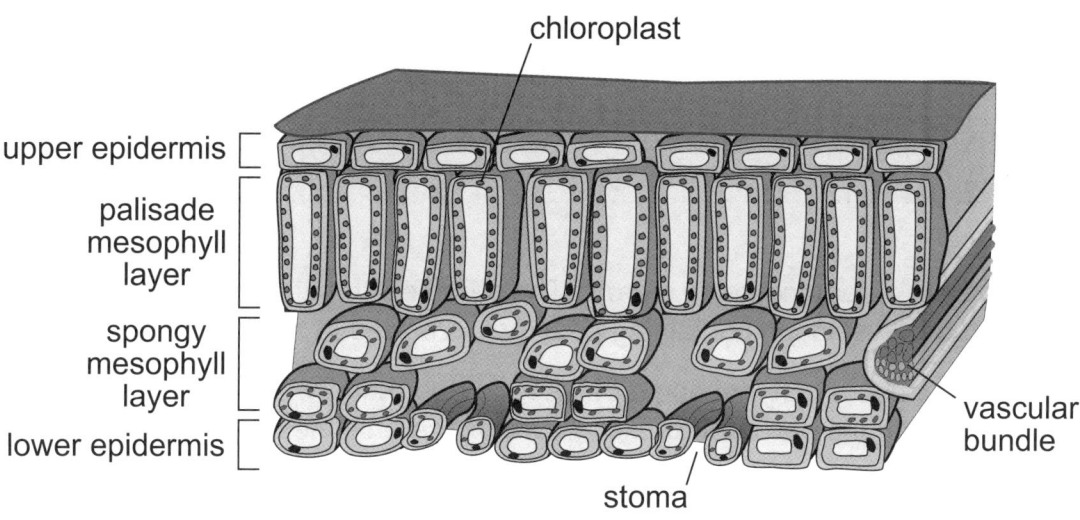

Light, water and carbon dioxide are all needed for photosynthesis, which takes place in the chloroplasts.

Use the diagram and your own knowledge to explain how the tissues in a leaf are adapted to maximise the efficiency of photosynthesis.

....

....

....

....

....

....

....

....

....

....

....

....

(6)

(Total for Question 7 = 6 marks)

8 Enzymes are important catalysts that speed up reactions in the body.

(a) (i) Name **two** enzymes that are involved in breaking down starch into glucose in the human body.

1. ....

2. ....

(2)

A sample of food contains starch. The sample is crushed and put into a test tube. A solution containing enzymes is added to the test tube.

(ii) Describe a test that could be used to determine whether or not the starch in the sample has been broken down by the enzymes.

....

....

....

(2)

(b) Fats are broken down in the small intestine by enzymes called lipases. This process is assisted by a fluid called bile, which is stored in the gall bladder.

(i) Which of the following organs produces bile?

☐ **A** liver

☐ **B** stomach

☐ **C** small intestine

☐ **D** gall bladder

(1)

(ii) Gallstones are small, solid objects that form in the gall bladder. They can block the bile ducts (tubes) that connect the gall bladder to the small intestine.

Suggest why somebody suffering from gallstones might digest fatty foods less efficiently than normal.

....

....

....

....

(4)

(c) The table shows the results of a student's investigation into the effect of temperature on the activity of the enzyme catalase, which catalyses the breakdown of hydrogen peroxide into water and oxygen.

The student measured the volume of oxygen produced within one minute when a source of catalase was added to hydrogen peroxide. She measured this at four different temperatures, repeating each test three times.

The results are shown in the table.

Temperature / °C	Volume of oxygen produced / cm³			
	Repeat 1	Repeat 2	Repeat 3	Mean
10	5.5	7.0	6.4	6.3
20	15.5	13.2	11.6	13.4
30	19.5	17.5	**X**	19.0
40	17.2	16.5	16.9	16.9

(i) Calculate the number that should be in the cell of the table labelled **X**.

.... cm³
(1)

(ii) Which of the following conclusions could the student draw from her results?

☐ **A** The optimum temperature for catalase is around 30 °C.

☐ **B** Above 20 °C, the active site of catalase changes shape so that it doesn't work as effectively.

☐ **C** As the temperature increases, catalase's activity increases.

☐ **D** Catalase works best at lower temperatures.

(1)

(Total for Question 8 = 11 marks)

9 The diagram below shows oxygen molecules moving into a cell through the cell membrane.

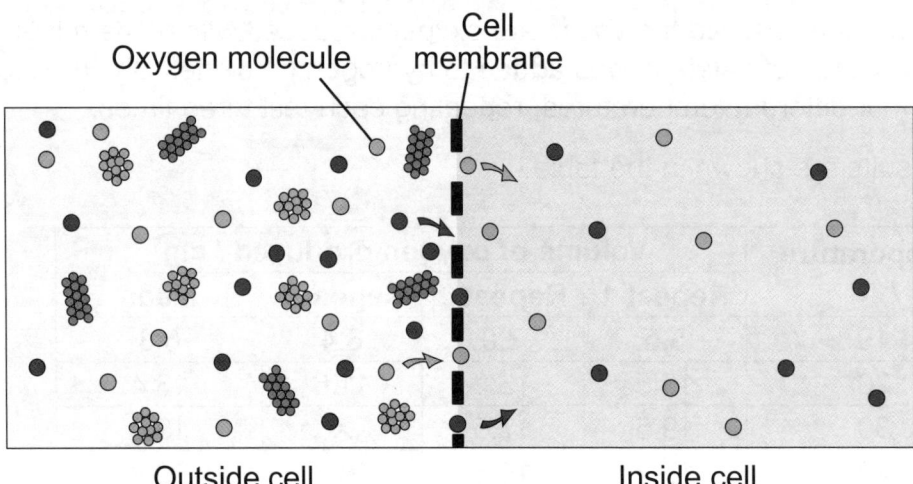

Outside cell   Inside cell

(a) Describe the process by which oxygen moves into cells.

....

....

....

....

(3)

(b) The rate of aerobic respiration increases inside the cell in the diagram.
Explain what will happen to the rate of oxygen movement across the cell membrane.

....

....

....

....

(3)

Trout are freshwater fish. They are relatively large, multicellular organisms. They have specialised organs that increase the efficiency of gas exchange.

Euglena are small, single-celled organisms that live in water. They do not have specialised gas exchange organs.

Both trout and *Euglena* need oxygen to survive.

(c) Suggest an explanation as to why *Euglena* do **not** need specialised organs for absorbing oxygen, but trout do.

....

....

....

....

....

....

....

(4)

17

(d) Yeast are single-celled organisms that can respire aerobically (with oxygen) or anaerobically (without oxygen).

Describe a method that you could use to investigate how the rate of anaerobic respiration in yeast is affected by temperature.

....

....

....

....

....

....

....

....

....

....

(5)

(Total for Question 9 = 15 marks)

10 There are a number of health problems that can result from smoking.
Tobacco smoke contains carcinogens, which are chemicals that can cause cancer.

A study compared the incidence of cancer per 100 000 men and the number of cigarettes they smoke per day. The results are shown in the table below.

Number of cigarettes smoked per day	Incidence of cancer per 100 000 men
10	50
20	120
30	230
40	420

(a) Complete the graph below, using the data from the table.
Draw a curve of best fit.

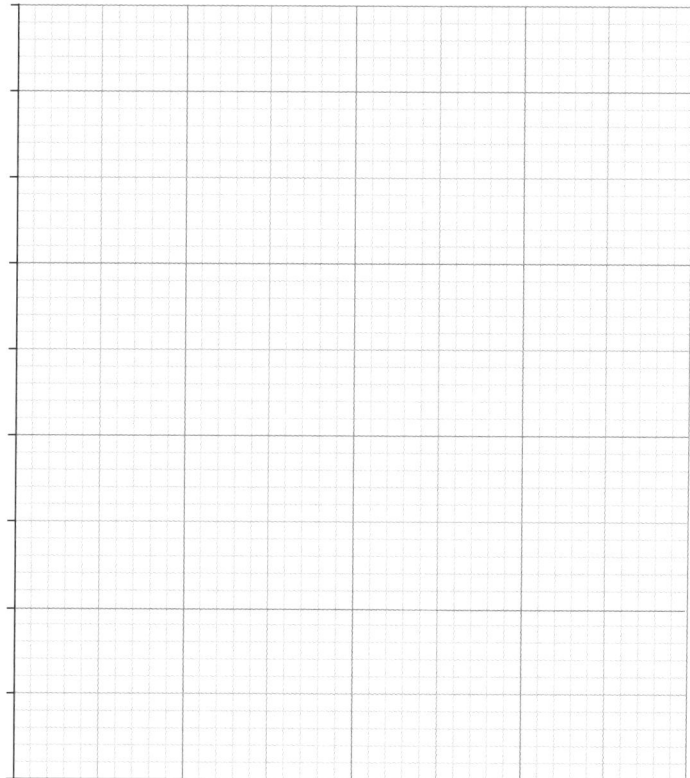

(4)

(b) A scientific magazine used the data in the table to report that people who smoke are more likely to die from cancer than people who don't smoke.

Does the data support this conclusion? Give reasons for your answer.

....

....

....

....

....

....

(3)

(Total for Question 10 = 7 marks)

20

11 The Earth's temperature is gradually increasing as a result of global warming.

(a) Explain how human activities are contributing to global warming.

....

....

....

....

....

....

....

....

....

....

....

....

(6)

(b) Which of the following is a cause of acid rain?

☐ **A** water pollution by sewage

☐ **B** eutrophication

☐ **C** air pollution by sulfur dioxide

☐ **D** air pollution by carbon dioxide

(1)

(Total for Question 11 = 7)

12 The diagram shows a human eye.

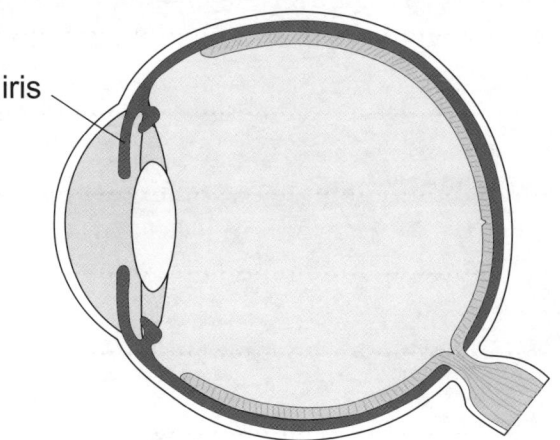

iris

(a) (i) Add labels to the diagram to show a **suspensory ligament** and the **retina**.

(2)

(ii) Explain how the structure of the iris relates to its function.

....

....

....

(2)

(iii) Explain how the eye adjusts to view **distant** objects.

....

....

....

....

....

(4)

(b) (i) A person sees something that is putting them in danger.
This triggers a hormonal response.

Name the hormone that is released, state its source in the body, and describe its effect on the body.

Hormone: ....

Source: ....

Effect: ....

....

....

(4)

(ii) Running away from the danger makes the person hot.

Give **two** ways that the skin will respond to this, and explain how each response helps to reduce the person's temperature.

1. ....

....

....

2. ....

....

....

(4)

(Total for Question 12 = 16)

TOTAL FOR PAPER = 110 MARKS

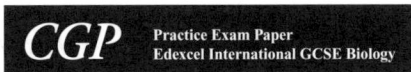

International GCSE Biology

Set A Paper 2

Centre name				
Centre number				
Candidate number				

Time allowed:
• 1 hour 15 minutes

Surname	
Other names	
Candidate signature	

Instructions to candidates
• Write your name and other details in the spaces provided above.
• Use a pen with black ink.
• You are allowed to use a calculator.
• Answer **all** questions in the spaces provided.
  There might be more space than you need.
• Answer multiple choice questions by putting a cross in the correct box.
  If you need to change your answer, draw a horizontal line through the box.
  Then mark your new answer as normal.

Information for candidates
• The marks available are given in brackets at the end of each question.
• There are 70 marks available for this paper.

Advice to candidates
• Try to answer all the questions.
• Carefully read each question before you try to answer it.
• If you have time at the end of the exam, check your answers.

For examiner's use

Q	Attempt N°			Q	Attempt N°		
	1	2	3		1	2	3
1				5			
2				6			
3				7			
4							
			Total				

Answer **all** questions in the spaces provided

1   Read the passage below, then answer the questions that follow.

Strawberry growing in the UK

strawberry plant   flower

1   Strawberries are an important food crop in the UK. Over 100 tonnes of strawberries are produced in the UK each year, and in recent years the amount of strawberries eaten there has been increasing. Strawberries are a good source of vitamin C, manganese and dietary fibre.

5   Strawberry plants can reproduce by putting out runners, which take root and grow into clones of their parent. Farmers who grow strawberries usually produce the new plants that they need by taking runners from mature strawberry plants and growing them in soil.

   New strawberry plants will produce fruit the year after they are planted.
10   After planting, they are usually fed with fertilisers and watered regularly. Many farmers also choose to treat their strawberry plants with chemical pesticides to kill pests. Some organic farms may choose to use biological control methods instead.

   Once the new strawberry plants have matured, they will start to flower.
15   Strawberry plants produce small, white flowers with bright yellow centres. These flowers produce nectar. Once the flowers are pollinated, the seeds will begin to develop, and then the berries will form. They grow in size and darken in colour until they become bright red. At this point, they are ready to be harvested.

20   Strawberry plants will grow outside in the UK, but most of the nation's crop is grown in polythene tunnels. Growing strawberries in a glasshouse or a polythene tunnel generally gives a higher yield than growing them in a field. Since glasshouses can be expensive to build and maintain, polythene tunnels are a cost effective way to get a good yield of fruit.

2

(a) Strawberry plants can reproduce by putting out runners, which take root and grow into clones of their parent (lines 5-6).

What is this type of reproduction called?

....

(1)

(b) Strawberries are a good source of dietary fibre (line 4).

Why is fibre important in a healthy diet?

☐ **A** It acts as a source of energy.

☐ **B** It helps your body to absorb calcium.

☐ **C** It is needed for the growth and repair of body tissues.

☐ **D** It aids the movement of food through the gut.

(1)

(c) Many farmers choose to treat their strawberry plants with pesticides to kill pests (lines 11-12).

Give **one** advantage and **two** disadvantages of farmers using chemical pesticides to treat their strawberry plants.

Advantage: ....

....

Disadvantage 1: ....

....

Disadvantage 2: ....

....

(3)

(d) Some organic farms use biological control methods instead of pesticides (lines 12-13).

What is meant by the term "biological control"?

....

....

(1)

3

(e) The flowers that develop on strawberry plants produce nectar (line 16).

Use this information to suggest how strawberry plants are pollinated.

....

(1)

(f) Once the strawberry plants have been pollinated, the seeds will begin to develop (lines 16-17).

Describe how pollination of the flower leads to seed formation.

....

....

....

....

....

(4)

(g) Growing strawberries in a glasshouse or a polythene tunnel generally gives a higher yield than growing them in a field (lines 21-22).

Give **two** reasons why growing strawberries in a glasshouse or a polythene tunnel generally gives higher yield than growing them in a field.

1. ....

....

2. ....

....

(2)

(Total for Question 1 = 13 marks)

4

2 Most cells in the human body contain chromosomes.

(a) Two chromosomes in each human body cell are sex chromosomes.
Describe how sex chromosomes differ between a male and a female.

....

....

(2)

Sperm cells only have one copy of each chromosome.

(b) Which process causes sperm cells to only have one copy of each chromosome?

☐ **A** differentiation

☐ **B** mitosis

☐ **C** meiosis

☐ **D** mutation

(1)

(c) During sexual reproduction, a sperm cell and an egg cell fuse together to form
a new cell. Describe how this new cell develops into a new organism.

....

....

....

....

(3)

(d) The DNA on the chromosomes in a cell acts as a code,
telling the cell how to make proteins.

Leave
blank

In the first part of this process, the DNA in the nucleus is used as a template
to create a complementary strand of mRNA.

Describe how a protein is made from the mRNA strand once it has been
produced in the nucleus.

....

....

....

....

....

....

....

....

....

....

....

....

(6)

(Total for Question 2 = 12 marks)

3 Blood is a vital part of the human circulatory system. It transports many substances, including oxygen and carbon dioxide, around the body.

(a) Which of the following statements about blood is correct?

☐ **A** Blood is a cell.

☐ **B** Blood is a tissue.

☐ **C** Blood is an organ.

☐ **D** Blood is an organ system.

(1)

(b) When a blood vessel is damaged, a blood clot forms to block the hole. Name **one** component of blood that is responsible for blood clotting.

....

(1)

(c) The function of red blood cells is to carry oxygen from the lungs to all of the cells in the body.

(i) Some athletes train in locations high above sea level for several weeks before a race. This increases the number of red blood cells the athletes have.

Even when the athletes have returned to locations nearer sea level, their red blood cell count can remain high for many days.

Suggest how training in locations high above sea level might improve an athlete's performance in a race.

....

....

....

....

....

....

(4)

(ii) Describe **one** way in which the structure of a red blood cell makes it well adapted for its function. Explain how the feature you have described helps it to perform its role effectively.

Feature: ....

....

Explanation: ....

....

(2)

(d) Blood flows around the body in blood vessels.
The diagram below shows two different types of blood vessel.

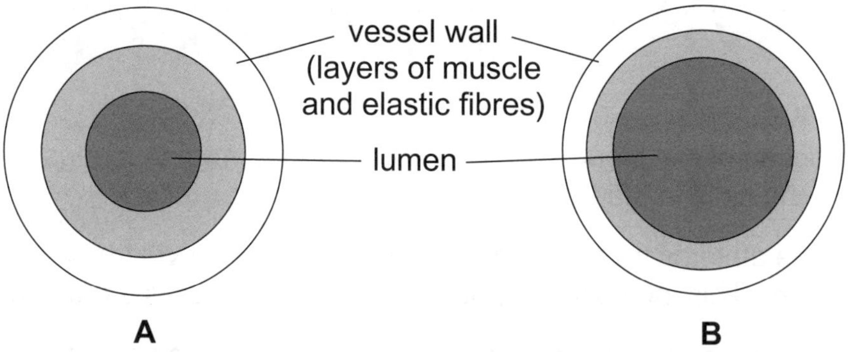

Name the type of blood vessel represented by **A** and **B** in the diagram above. Give a reason for each of your choices.

Blood vessel **A**: ....

Reason:..

Blood vessel **B**: ....

Reason: ....

(2)

(Total for Question 3 = 10 marks)

4 A student is investigating osmosis using Visking tubing.
Visking tubing is a partially permeable membrane.
Water can pass through Visking tubing, but large sugar molecules cannot.

The diagram below shows the student's apparatus at the start of her investigation.

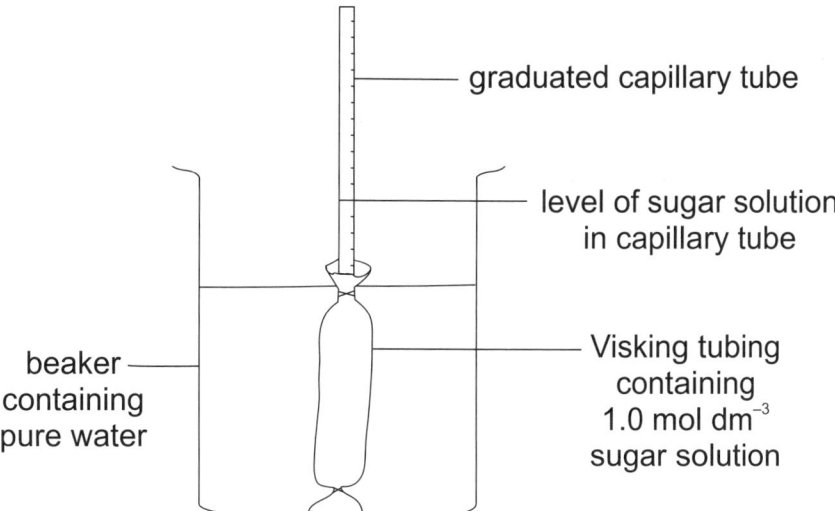

The student leaves the apparatus for 30 minutes.

(a) Suggest what will happen to the volume of the sugar solution inside the
    capillary tube during this time period. Explain your answer in terms of osmosis.

....

....

....

....

(3)

(b) Suggest how the student could modify her experiment to investigate
    the effect of changing the concentration gradient on the rate of osmosis.

....

....

....

....

....

(3)

(c) A second student investigated osmosis using potato pieces.

He cut three equally sized cubes from a raw potato. He measured the mass of each cube. Then he placed all three cubes in a concentrated salt solution.

After 6 hours, he took the potato cubes out, dried them, and then measured their mass again. His results are shown in the table below.

	Cube 1	Cube 2	Cube 3
Mass at start of experiment / g	9.6	9.7	9.5
Mass after 6 hours / g	8.4	8.2	8.3
Change in mass / g	−1.2	−1.5	−1.2

(i) Calculate the mean change in mass of the three potato cubes.

mean change in mass = ... g

(1)

(ii) The student repeated the experiment using a smaller cube of potato, but keeping all the other variables the same. This time the mass of the potato cube changed from 6.2 g to 5.1 g.

Calculate the percentage change in the mass of this potato cube during the experiment. Give your answer to two significant figures.

percentage change = ... %

(2)

(Total for Question 4 = 9 marks)

5 The diagram below shows the blood water content of a person over a period of several hours.

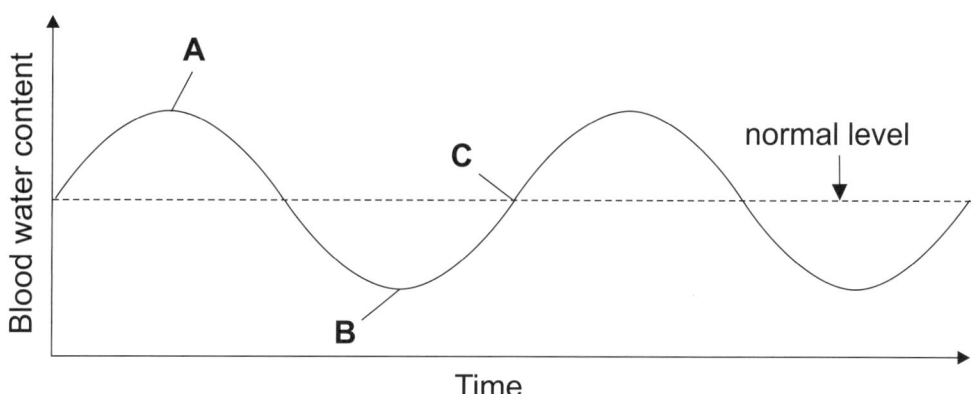

(a) Name the point, **A**, **B** or **C**, at which the hormone ADH is most likely to be released. Explain your answer.

Point at which ADH is most likely to be released ....

Explanation ....

....

....

....

(3)

(b) (i) Name the gland that ADH is released from.

....

(1)

(ii) Describe the effect that the release of ADH will have on the concentration of the person's urine.

....

....

(1)

(Total for Question 5 = 5 marks)

6 In 1996, scientists at the Roslin Institute in Edinburgh cloned a sheep. The sheep, Dolly, was the first mammal ever to be successfully cloned using an adult body cell.

(a) Describe the process used to produce Dolly the sheep.

....

....

....

....

....

....

....

....

....

....

(5)

Plants with desirable characteristics can be cloned using micropropagation.

(b) A scientist has taken some explants from the side shoots of a plant. After sterilising them, she places them on to a growing medium in a Petri dish.

Name **two** things that the growing medium in the Petri dish should contain in order to help the cloned plants to develop successfully.

1. ....

2. ....

(2)

(Total for Question 6 = 7 marks)

12

7 Plants lose water through the stomata in their leaves.

A student set up an experiment to show that more water is lost from the lower surface of a leaf than from the upper surface.

He used cobalt chloride paper in his experiment.
This paper is blue when it is dry and pink when it is wet.

This is the method he used:

1.   He took a potted plant and taped a piece of dry cobalt chloride paper to the upper surface of one of the plant's leaves.

2.   He taped a second piece of paper to the lower surface of the same leaf.

3.   He left the plant for 5 minutes.

4.   He observed the colour of the pieces of cobalt chloride paper.

The results of his experiment are shown in the table below.

	Colour of paper at start of experiment	Colour of paper after 5 minutes
Upper surface of leaf	blue	blue
Lower surface of leaf	blue	pink

(a) Suggest an explanation for the results shown in the table.

....

....

....

....

(3)

(b) The student repeated the experiment on a different day.
This time, neither piece of cobalt chloride paper turned pink after 5 minutes.

Suggest why the results of this experiment may be different on different days.

....

....

....

(2)

It is assumed that water loss from the leaves of a plant is directly proportional to water uptake from the roots.

A student carried out an investigation to assess the rate of water uptake by a plant over a 24-hour period. The results are shown in the graph below.

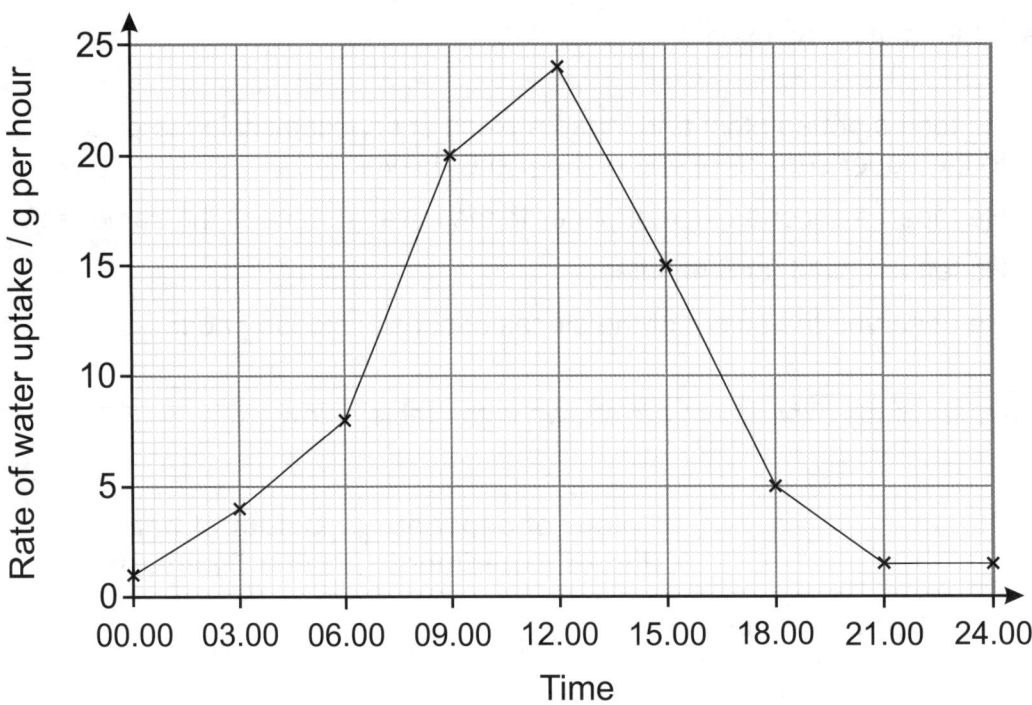

(c) (i) Stomata are small. It is difficult to accurately measure their diameter unless they are fully open.

Use the graph to suggest what time of day it would be best to measure the diameter of stomata on leaves. Give an explanation for your suggestion.

....

....

....

....

(3)

(ii) Suggest an explanation for the changes in the rate of water uptake shown in the graph.

....

....

....

....

....

....

(4)

(iii) To calculate the rate of water uptake by the plant, the student used this formula.

$$\text{rate of water uptake (g/hour)} = \frac{\text{change in mass of plant (g)}}{\text{time (hours)}}$$

Between 21.00 (9 p.m.) and 24.00 (midnight), the rate of water uptake of the plant stayed constant at 1.5 g/hour. Use this information to calculate the change in the mass of the plant during this time period.

change in mass of plant = ... g

(2)

(Total for Question 7 = 14 marks)

TOTAL FOR PAPER = 70 MARKS

15

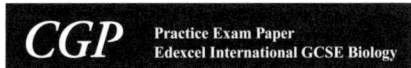
International GCSE Biology

Set B Paper 1

In addition to this paper you should have:
- A ruler.
- A calculator.

Centre name				
Centre number				
Candidate number				

Surname	
Other names	
Candidate signature	

Time allowed:
- 2 hours

Instructions to candidates
- Write your name and other details in the spaces provided above.
- Use a pen with black ink.
- You are allowed to use a calculator.
- Answer **all** questions in the spaces provided.
  There might be more space than you need.
- Answer multiple choice questions by putting a cross in the correct box.
  If you need to change your answer, draw a horizontal line through the box.
  Then mark your new answer as normal.

Information for candidates
- The marks available are given in brackets
  at the end of each question.
- There are 110 marks available for this paper.

Advice to candidates
- Try to answer all the questions.
- Carefully read each question before you try to answer it.
- If you have time at the end of the exam, check your answers.

For examiner's use

Q	Attempt Nº 1	2	3	Q	Attempt Nº 1	2	3
1				8			
2				9			
3				10			
4				11			
5				12			
6				13			
7				Total			

1 An ecosystem is affected by both biotic and abiotic factors.

(a) Which of the following statements is correct?

☐ **A** Biotic factors include soil pH, wind direction and moisture levels.

☐ **B** Abiotic factors include competition, predators and temperature.

☐ **C** Abiotic factors include soil pH, wind direction and moisture levels.

☐ **D** Biotic factors include competition, predators and temperature.

(1)

Below are some photographs of organisms within a coastal community.

Puffin

Herring

Zooplankton

(b) Puffins feed on the herring. The herring feed on the zooplankton.

(i) Suggest what effect the removal of a large number of herring may have on the number of **puffins** in the community. Explain your answer.

....

....

....

(2)

(ii) Suggest what effect the removal of a large number of herring may have on the number of **zooplankton** in the community. Explain your answer.

....

....

....

(2)

(Total for Question 1 = 5 marks)

2

2 The brain makes up part of the central nervous system.

(a) Name the other part of the central nervous system.

....

(1)

(b) Which of the following statements about how nervous responses are different from hormonal responses is correct?

☐ **A** Nervous responses are slower and act for a longer time.

☐ **B** Nervous responses are slower and act on a less precise area.

☐ **C** Nervous responses act for a longer time and on a more precise area.

☐ **D** Nervous responses act for a shorter time and on a more precise area.

(1)

The diagram shows a reflex arc involved in the response when a person touches a hot object.

(c) Use the diagram to explain what happens when a person touches a hot object.

....

....

....

....

....

....

(4)

(Total for Question 2 = 6 marks)

3   Tuberculosis is a disease caused by a bacterium.

(a) Which of the following is **not** a feature of a typical bacterial cell?

☐ **A**   nucleus

☐ **B**   cell wall

☐ **C**   plasmid

☐ **D**   cell membrane

(1)

(b) Tuberculosis can be treated with the antibiotics isoniazid and rifampicin.

However, these antibiotics do not work in people who have been infected by certain strains of the tuberculosis bacterium.

Suggest how these bacterial strains developed.

....

....

....

....

....

....

(4)

(Total for Question 3 = 5 marks)

4 A student decided to investigate how respiring seeds affect the temperature of their surroundings.

The diagram shows how the student set up her experiment.

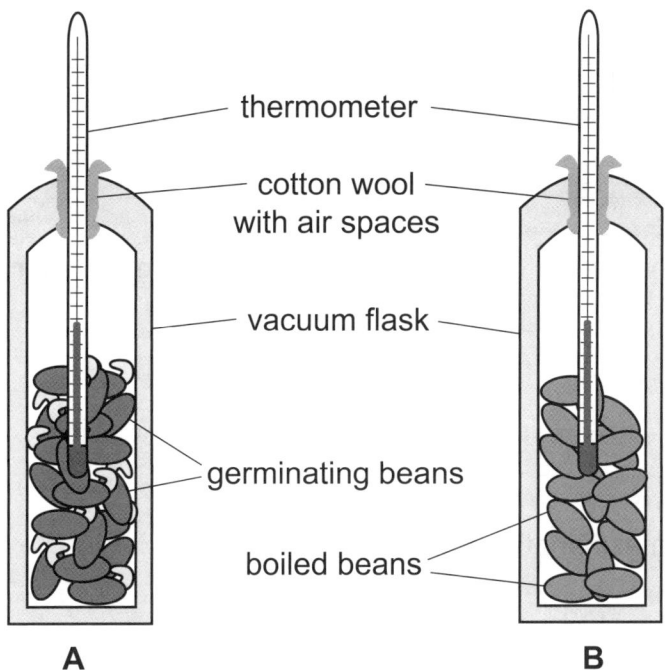

thermometer

cotton wool with air spaces

vacuum flask

germinating beans

boiled beans

A   **B**

The temperature inside the flasks was recorded on day 1 of the experiment, immediately after the beans had been added to the flasks.

The temperature inside the flasks was then recorded every day at the same time for another 4 days.

(a) Suggest why the flasks are sealed with cotton wool rather than rubber bungs.

....

....

(1)

The table shows the results of the experiment.

	Temperature / °C	
Day	Flask A	Flask B
1	18	18
2	20	19
3	21	18
4	24	19
5	26	19

(b) (i) Describe the overall trend in results shown in the table for flask **A**.

....

....

(1)

(ii) Suggest an explanation for the flask **A** results.

....

....

....

(2)

(c) Suggest why boiled beans were used in flask **B** in the experiment.

....

....

....

....

(3)

(Total for Question 4 = 7 marks)

6

5 Humans can use techniques such as selective breeding and genetic engineering to produce organisms with desired characteristics.

Many different types of fruit are produced by selective breeding.

A farmer grows several different varieties of raspberry plant on her farm.

The table shows some of the characteristics of these raspberry plants. Each characteristic is partly controlled by the plants' genes.

Raspberry Plant Variety	Fruit Characteristics				
	Size	**Firmness**	**Taste**	**Shelf-life**	**Yield**
A	Large	Soft	Sour	Short	High
B	Medium	Hard	Sweet	Short	Low
C	Small	Hard	Sweet	Long	Medium

(a) The farmer would like to produce a plant that has these characteristics:

- Large fruit
- Soft fruit
- Sweet taste
- Long shelf-life
- High yield

(i) Suggest which **two** raspberry plant varieties from the table should be bred together to produce the desired characteristics.

....

(1)

(ii) Describe how the farmer would use the selected raspberry plants to produce plants with the desired characteristics.

....

....

....

....

....

....

(3)

(b) Crop plants with desirable characteristics can also be produced by genetic engineering.

    (i) Describe how enzymes and vectors can be used to genetically engineer a plant in order to increase food production.

....

....

....

....

....

....

....

....

....

....

....

(6)

    (ii) Genetic engineering is also useful in medicine.

Describe **one** way that genetic engineering is carried out for medical purposes.

....

....

....

(2)

(Total for Question 5 = 12 marks)

6 Breathing ventilates the lungs for gas exchange.

(a) Gas exchange happens via diffusion.
Which of the following is the correct definition of diffusion?

☐ **A** The movement of gas molecules in any direction.

☐ **B** The spreading out of particles in a solution or gas from an area of higher concentration to an area of lower concentration.

☐ **C** The spreading out of particles in a solution or gas from an area of lower concentration to an area of higher concentration.

☐ **D** The movement of substances from a more dilute solution to a more concentrated solution, which requires energy.

(1)

The diagram shows some alveoli in the human lungs.

alveoli

capillaries

(b) Give **two** ways in which the alveoli are adapted to carry out the process of gas exchange.

Explain how each of these adaptations improves the efficiency of gas exchange.

1. ....

....

2. ....

....

(4)

(c) (i) When a person breathes in, air passes through the structures in the thorax. Put the following structures in the order that this air reaches them: bronchiole, bronchus, alveolus, trachea.

....

(1)

(ii) Which of the following correctly describes what happens when a person breathes in?

☐ **A** The intercostal muscles relax, the diaphragm relaxes, the thorax volume increases.

☐ **B** The intercostal muscles contract, the diaphragm contracts, the thorax volume increases.

☐ **C** The intercostal muscles contract, the diaphragm relaxes, the thorax volume decreases.

☐ **D** The intercostal muscles relax, the diaphragm contracts, the thorax volume decreases.

(1)

(d) An exercise bike has a variable speed setting, meaning the speed a person has to cycle on it can be changed.

Describe an experiment you could carry out to test the following prediction:
'The faster a person is cycling, the faster their breathing rate will be.'

....

....

....

....

....

....

....

....

....

....

(5)

(Total for Question 6 = 12 marks)

7 The table shows the dimensions of three cubes, **A**, **B** and **C**. Each cube represents a different single-celled organism that lives in a freshwater pond.
The cubes are not drawn to scale.

	A	B	C
Cube dimensions / mm	0.5 × 0.5 × 0.5	0.1 × 0.1 × 0.1	0.3 × 0.3 × 0.3
Surface area / mm²	**X**	0.06	0.54
Volume / mm³	0.125	**Y**	0.027
Surface area : volume	12:1	60:1	**Z**

(a) Calculate the values of **X**, **Y** and **Z** in the table.

X = ... mm²

Y = ... mm³

Z = ... : 1

(3)

(b) How many times bigger is the surface area to volume ratio of cube **B** than that of cube **A**?

....

(1)

The organisms represented by the cubes in the table all need to exchange substances with their environment.

(c) Which cube (**A**, **B** or **C**) represents the organism with the slowest rate of exchange? Explain your answer.

Cube: ....

Explanation: ....

....

(2)

(d) Explain how the temperature of the pond water could affect the rate at which the organisms exchange substances with their environment.

....

....

....

(2)

Two of the cubes in the table represent protoctists.

(e) (i) Name **one** example of a single-celled protoctist that lives in pond water.

....

(1)

(ii) Name a type of eukaryotic organism, other than protoctists, that can be single-celled.

....

(1)

(Total for Question 7 = 10 marks)

8 Humans must grow and develop in order to reach adulthood.

The diagram shows a fetus in a uterus.

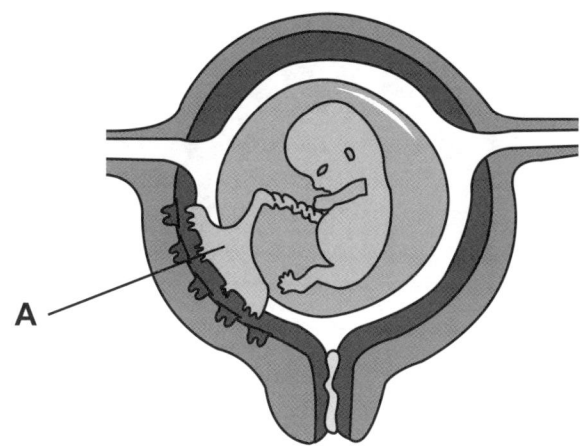

A

(a) (i) Give the name and function of the feature labelled **A** in the diagram.

Name: ....

Function: ....

....

(2)

(ii) Name the fluid that protects the fetus as it develops.

....

(1)

(b) Draw a genetic diagram to show how there is an equal chance that the sex of a baby will be male or female.

(2)

(c) The level of testosterone in a young boy's body is starting to increase.

(i) Give **two** changes that this will bring about.

1. ....

2. ....

(1)

(ii) Name the component of the blood that is responsible for transporting testosterone around the body.

....

(1)

(Total for Question 8 = 7 marks)

9 Photosynthesis is a reaction which occurs in the leaves of a plant.

(a) Complete the symbol equation for photosynthesis below.

$$6CO_2 \;+\; 6H_2O \;\longrightarrow\; C_6H_{12}O_6 \;+\; \dots\dots\dots$$

(1)

The rate of photosynthesis has several limiting factors. These are factors that stop photosynthesis from happening any faster.

The graph shows the effect of light intensity on the rate of photosynthesis.

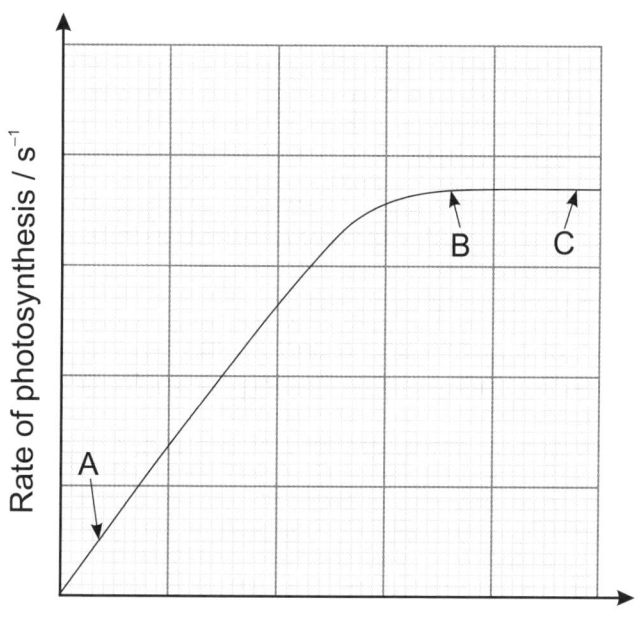

Light intensity / arbitrary units

(b) Between which points on the graph, if any, is light intensity the limiting factor on the rate of photosynthesis?

    ☐   **A**   A and B

    ☐   **B**   A and C

    ☐   **C**   B and C

    ☐   **D**   never

(1)

The graph below shows the effect of light intensity and carbon dioxide on the rate of photosynthesis.

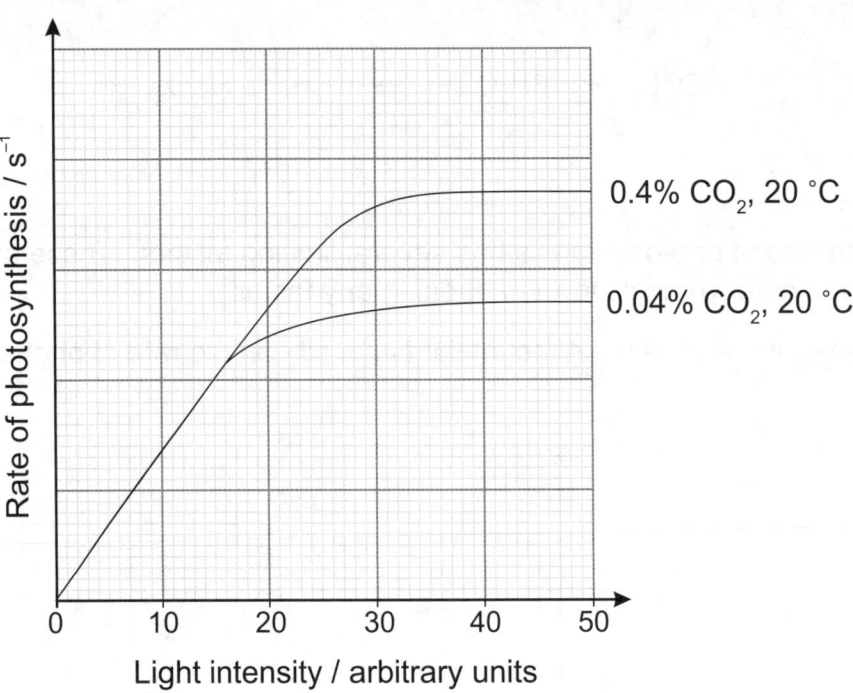

0.4% CO_2, 20 °C

0.04% CO_2, 20 °C

Light intensity / arbitrary units

(c) A student looks at this graph and says:
'At a light intensity of 30 units and a carbon dioxide concentration of 0.04%, carbon dioxide concentration is the limiting factor for photosynthesis.'

Describe the evidence from the graph which supports this statement.

....

....

....

....

(2)

A student investigated the effect of light intensity on the rate of photosynthesis in pondweed. He varied the light intensity by changing the distance of the pondweed from a lamp. He measured the rate of photosynthesis by counting the number of bubbles of oxygen the pondweed produced in one minute.

The results from the experiment are shown in the table.

Distance from lamp / cm	Number of bubbles per minute
5	53
10	45
20	34
30	27
40	23

(d) (i) Complete the graph below using the results in the table.
Draw a curve of best fit.

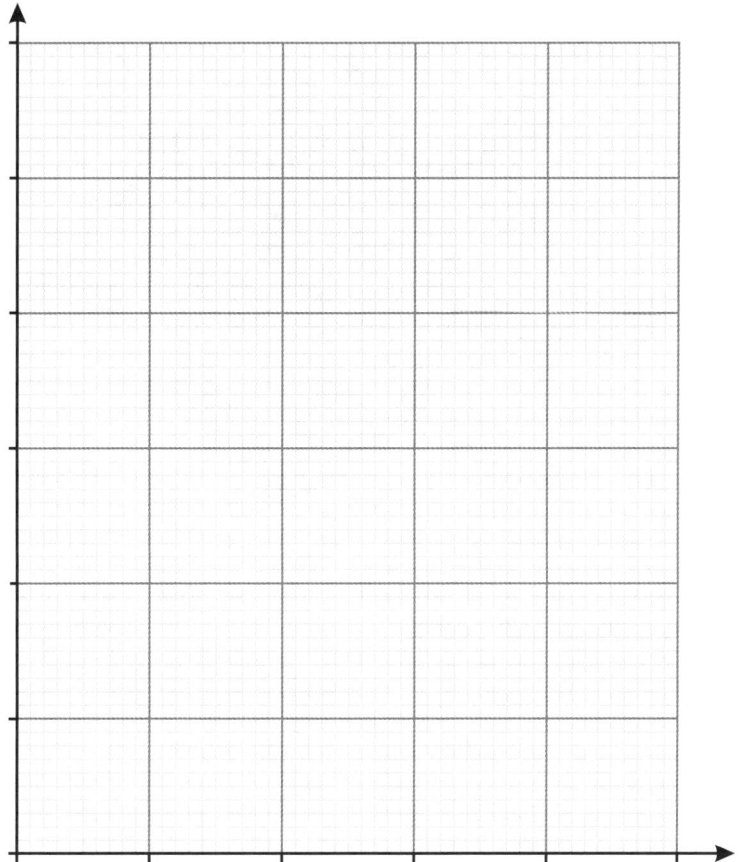

(4)

(ii) Use the graph above to estimate the distance the lamp would have to be from the beaker for 32 bubbles per minute to have been produced.

Distance = ... cm

(1)

(iii) Give a conclusion that the student could draw from these results.

....

....

....

(2)

(Total for Question 9 = 11 marks)

10 The diagram shows a human heart.

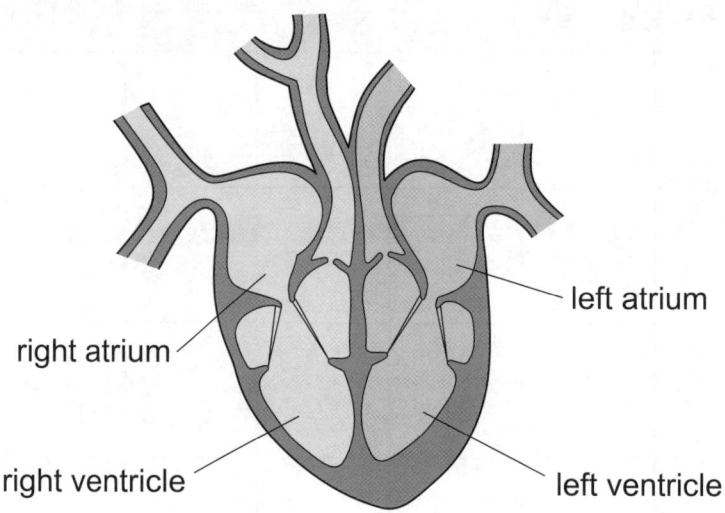

Use the diagram and your own knowledge to describe how blood flows through the left and right sides of the heart.

....

....

....

....

....

....

....

....

....

....

....

....

(Total for Question 10 = 6 marks)

11 The image shows a dog.

Respiration transfers energy from the dog's food to the cells in its body.

Some of the energy transferred by respiration is used to build up larger molecules from smaller molecules.

(a) State which smaller molecules make up a lipid molecule.

....

(1)

Respiration can take place aerobically or anaerobically.

(b) Describe the differences between aerobic and anaerobic respiration in animals.

....

....

....

....

....

(3)

(c) Dog food contains a mix of essential nutrients, including protein and fats.

(i) A student prepared a sample of dog food for testing.

Describe how the student could test for the presence of proteins in the prepared sample.

....

....

....

(2)

(ii) Dogs have a similar digestive system to humans.
Suggest and explain how a dog may digest a meal containing fats.

....

....

....

....

....

....

(4)

(Total for Question 11 = 10 marks)

20

12 Guinea pigs can have rough or smooth hair.

The gene that controls hair type has two alleles. Rough hair is controlled by the allele 'R' and smooth hair is controlled by the allele 'r'.

The diagram shows a genetic cross between two rough-haired guinea pigs.

Parents' genotypes: (Rr)   (Rr)

Meiosis

Gametes' genotypes: (R) (r) (R) (r)

Fertilisation

Offspring's genotypes: (RR) (Rr) (Rr) (rr)

(a) Use the genetic diagram to explain what happens to the number of chromosomes during meiosis and fertilisation.

....

....

....

....

....

....

(4)

(b) What is the expected ratio of rough-haired guinea pigs to smooth-haired guinea pigs in the offspring of the cross shown in the genetic diagram?

....

(1)

21

A heterozygous female guinea pig was crossed with a male guinea pig homozygous for smooth hair. They had a litter of 6 offspring.

(c) Calculate the number of offspring you would expect to have smooth hair.

Complete the genetic diagram below to explain your answer.

Expected number of offspring with smooth hair: ....

(5)

(d) Describe how the way in which hair type is determined in guinea pigs differs from the way in which inheritance works for most phenotypic features.

....

....

....

(1)

(Total for Question 12 = 11 marks)

13 Plants require mineral ions for healthy growth.
They absorb these ions from the soil into their roots.

Mineral ions are present in low concentrations in the soil.
They are absorbed into cells in the plant's roots by active transport.

(a) Use the information above to explain why cells in the plant's roots contain
many mitochondria.

....

....

....

(2)

Plants can be damaged by mineral ion deficiencies.

A student set up an experiment to determine the effect of mineral ion deficiencies
on the growth of plants.

He took two seedlings and placed each one into a test tube.
This is shown in the diagram.

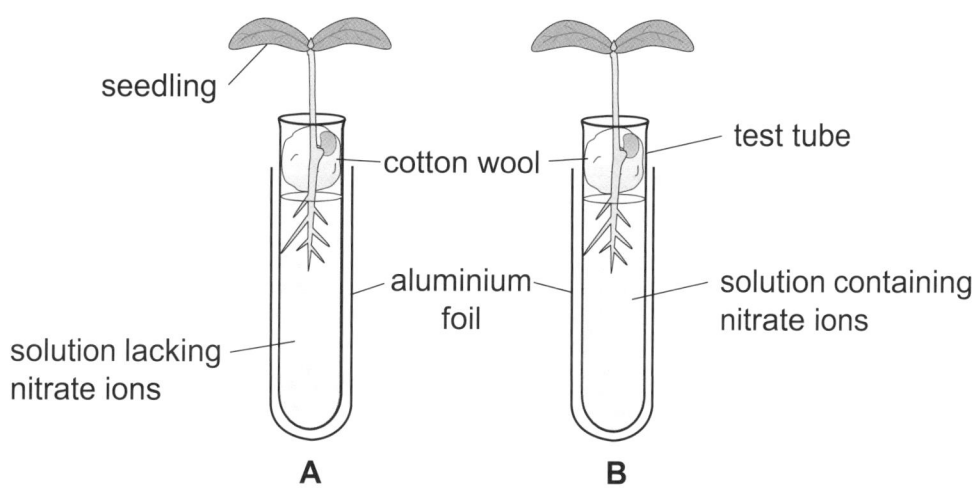

The test tubes were wrapped in a layer of aluminium foil to exclude light and to
prevent algae from growing in the solution.

The seedlings were left to grow in these solutions for four weeks, during which
time the level of water in the test tubes was kept topped up with distilled water.

After four weeks the condition of the plants was recorded.

(b) Suggest why it was important to stop algae growing in the solutions.

....

....

....

(2)

(c) Suggest **one** difference you would expect to see between the seedlings in test tubes **A** and **B** after four weeks. Explain your answer.

Difference: ....

....

Explanation: ....

....

(3)

(d) After two weeks, the seedlings in both test tubes **A** and **B** were unable to make chlorophyll.

Suggest why.

....

....

(1)

(Total for Question 13 = 8 marks)

TOTAL FOR PAPER = 110 MARKS

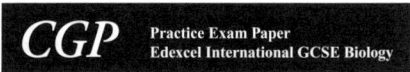

International GCSE Biology

Set B Paper 2

In addition to this paper you should have:
- A ruler.
- A calculator.

Centre name				
Centre number				
Candidate number				

Surname	
Other names	
Candidate signature	

Time allowed:
- 1 hour 15 minutes

Instructions to candidates
- Write your name and other details in the spaces provided above.
- Use a pen with black ink.
- You are allowed to use a calculator.
- Answer **all** questions in the spaces provided.
  There might be more space than you need.
- Answer multiple choice questions by putting a cross in the correct box.
  If you need to change your answer, draw a horizontal line through the box.
  Then mark your new answer as normal.

Information for candidates
- The marks available are given in brackets at the end of each question.
- There are 70 marks available for this paper.

Advice to candidates
- Try to answer all the questions.
- Carefully read each question before you try to answer it.
- If you have time at the end of the exam, check your answers.

For examiner's use

Q	Attempt Nº			Q	Attempt Nº		
	1	2	3		1	2	3
1				5			
2				6			
3				7			
4							
		Total					

1   Read the passage below, then answer the questions that follow.

Stem cells in medicine

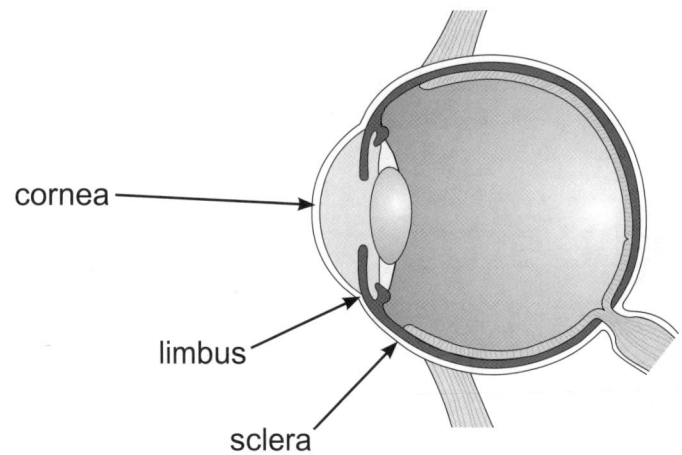

cornea

limbus

sclera

1   Most cells in the human body are specialised. Stem cells are
     unspecialised cells. They are found in early human embryos, where
     they have the potential to divide and produce any specialised cell type.
     They are also found in a limited number of places in the adult body,
5   including the bone marrow.

     The use of stem cells to cure disease is an important area of medical
     research. One treatment that is already in use involves stem cells
     taken from an area of the eye between the cornea and the sclera,
     called the limbus. If a patient's cornea becomes damaged, but the
10   limbus in at least one of their eyes remains intact, stem cells can be
     taken from the limbus and used to repair the damaged cornea. This
     can allow the patient to see clearly again. Patients without an intact
     limbus are unable to benefit from this treatment.

     Researchers are also investigating whether stem cells could be used
15   to replace neurones in the spinal cord that have been damaged or
     destroyed due to injury. Injuries to the spinal cord can damage both
     sensory and motor neurones, resulting in loss of sensation and full
     or partial paralysis (the inability to move muscles) for the patient.
     The spinal cord does not have its own source of stem cells. However,
20   scientists have investigated treatments that use adult stem cells from
     other areas of the body, as well as embryonic stem cells.

(a) Most cells in the human body are specialised (line 1).
Describe what is meant by a specialised cell.

....

....

(1)

(b) Stem cells are found in early human embryos (line 2).
Name the cell produced at fertilisation, which divides to form the stem cells of
an early human embryo.

....

(1)

(c) Stem cells from the limbus can be used to repair a damaged
cornea and allow a patient to see clearly again (lines 10-12).

(i) Explain why a damaged cornea may prevent a person from being able
to see.

....

....

....

....

(3)

(ii) Suggest how stem cells taken from the limbus could be used to repair
the cornea.

....

....

....

....

(3)

3

(d) (i) Injuries to the spinal cord can damage both sensory and motor neurones, resulting in loss of sensation and full or partial paralysis (the inability to move muscles) (lines 16-18).

Suggest how injuries to the sensory and motor neurones could cause these symptoms.

....

....

....

....

....

(4)

(ii) Scientists have investigated using both adult stem cells and embryonic stem cells to treat spinal cord injuries (lines 20-21).

Give **one** advantage and **one** disadvantage of the use of embryonic stem cells over adult stem cells in this treatment.

Advantage: ....

....

Disadvantage: ....

....

(2)

(Total for Question 1 = 14 marks)

2 Plants exchange gases for respiration and photosynthesis through their stomata.

(a) Which of the following is the correctly balanced symbol equation for aerobic respiration in plants?

☐ **A** $6CO_2 + 6H_2O \rightarrow C_6H_{12}O_6 + 6O_2$

☐ **B** $C_6H_{12}O_6 + 6O_2 \rightarrow 6CO_2 + 6H_2O$

☐ **C** $C_6H_{12}O_6 + O_2 \rightarrow CO_2 + H_2O$

☐ **D** $C_6H_{12}O_6 \rightarrow 2C_2H_5OH + 2CO_2$

(1)

(b) Explain how and why the net gas exchange of a plant changes over the course of a typical 24-hour period.

....

....

....

....

....

....

....

....

....

....

....

(6)

(Total for Question 2 = 7 marks)

3   Fish can be farmed as a source of protein for humans.

(a) Which of the following describes the function of protein as a component of the diet?

☐ **A**   Aids calcium absorption.

☐ **B**   Aids the movement of food through the gut.

☐ **C**   Needed for the growth and repair of tissue.

☐ **D**   Acts as an energy store and provides insulation.

(1)

(b) Some fish are farmed at sea in cages like the ones in this photograph.

(i) Explain how these cages protect the fish from both interspecific and intraspecific predation.

....

....

....

....

(2)

(ii) Besides protection from predation, suggest and explain **one** reason why the fish in these cages may grow bigger than fish of the same species living in open water.

....

....

....

....

(2)

(c) Fish farms can reduce local water quality, as the waste produced by fish contains nitrates. Water quality can also be reduced by local sewage outlets.

Explain the biological consequences that can occur as a result of pollution from a sewage outlet.

....

....

....

....

....

....

....

....

....

(5)

(Total for Question 3 = 10 marks)

4 A DNA molecule is made up of two strands coiled together in a double helix.

(a) The bases that connect the two strands in a DNA molecule always pair up in the same way.

A section of DNA was analysed.
24% of its nucleotides were found to contain base **A**.

Calculate the percentage of nucleotides in this section of DNA that you would expect to contain base **C**.

Nucleotides that contain base C = ...%

(3)

A mutation is a random change in an organism's DNA.

(b) The diagram below shows the normal order of bases in a section of DNA and then the same section of DNA after a mutation has occurred.

DNA before mutation: T A C T T T A C C
DNA after mutation: T A C T T A A C C

The table below shows four DNA base sequences along with the amino acid that each sequence codes for.

DNA base sequence	Amino acid coded for
TTA	asparagine
ACC	tryptophan
TTT	lysine
TAC	methionine

(i) Using the information in the diagram and the table above, write down the order of amino acids coded for **after** the mutation has taken place.

....

....

(1)

(ii) The section of DNA in the diagram codes for part of a protein.
Explain why the mutation shown alters the protein that is produced.

....

....

(1)

(c) State **two** ways in which the incidence of mutations can be increased.

1. ....

2. ....

(2)

(d) Explain why most mutations are not harmful to an organism.

....

....

....

....

(2)

(Total for Question 4 = 9 marks)

5 The enzyme amylase breaks down starch into simple sugars.

A student investigated the effect of pH on the rate at which amylase breaks down starch. This is the method she used:

1. Amylase and starch solution were added to six test tubes, each of which contained a different pH buffer solution.

2. Spotting tiles were prepared with one drop of iodine solution in each well.

3. Every 30 seconds, a sample of the amylase and starch solution was removed from the test tube and placed in a well on one of the spotting tiles.

4. The colour of the solution in the well was observed.

5. When all the starch had been broken down, the time was recorded.

6. The experiment was repeated three times for each of the six solutions.

7. A mean time and rate of reaction was calculated for each solution.

The student's results are shown in the table below.

pH of buffer solution	Time taken for starch to be broken down by amylase / s				Mean rate of reaction / s^{-1}
	Repeat 1	Repeat 2	Repeat 3	Mean	
4	510	600	570	560	1.8
5	420	450	390	420	2.4
6	150	120	180	150	6.7
7	180	120	150	150	6.7
8	240	210	240	230	4.3
9	330	270	330	310	3.2

(a) Explain how the student would have known when all the starch had been broken down by the amylase.

....

....

....

(2)

(b) (i) Complete the graph below to show the data in the table.
Join the points with straight lines.

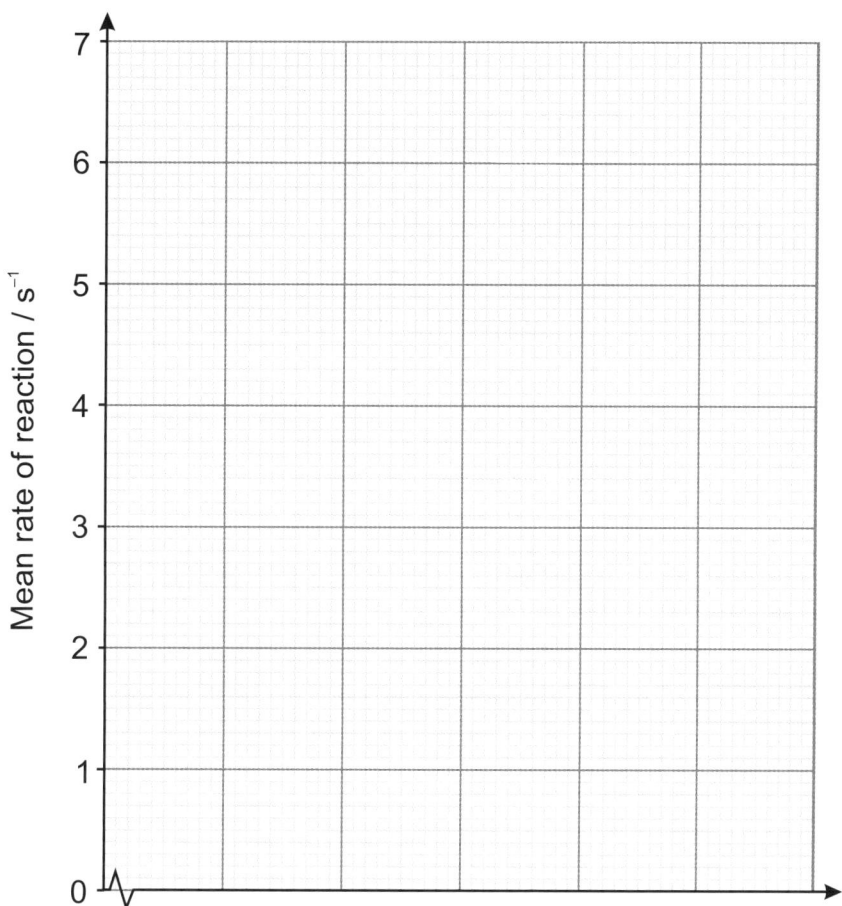

(4)

(ii) Use your graph to estimate the rate of reaction at **pH 5.5**.

Rate of reaction = ... s⁻¹
(1)

(c) The results for the mean rate of reaction at pH 6 and 7 are the same.
Suggest how the experiment could be improved to determine the optimum pH
for amylase more accurately.

....

....

(1)

(d) Give a conclusion that can be drawn from the results about the effect of pH on the rate of amylase activity.

....

....

(1)

(e) Explain why changing the pH affects enzyme activity.

....

....

....

(2)

(f) Amylase is produced in the salivary glands of the mouth and in the small intestine. Describe how the mouth is connected to the small intestine.

....

....

....

(2)

(Total for Question 5 = 13 marks)

6 The diagram below shows the urinary system.

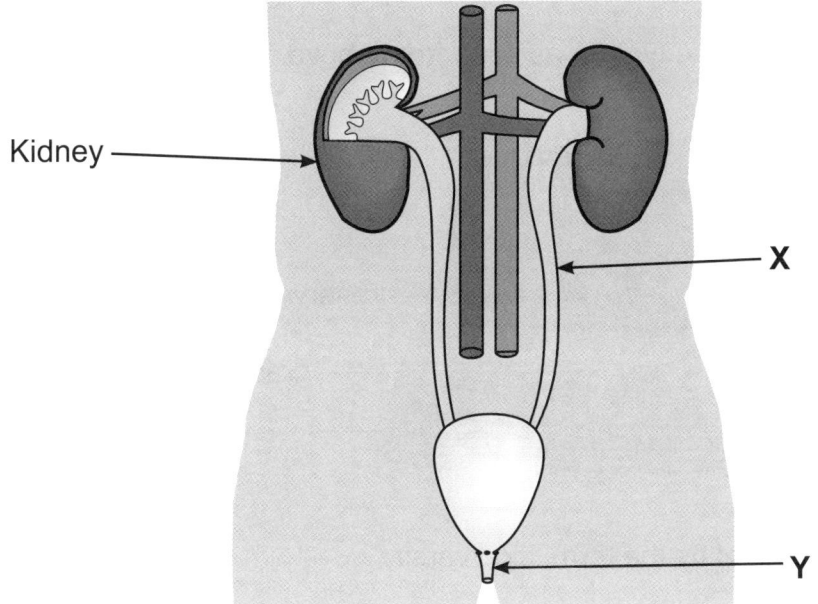

Kidney

X

Y

(a) Name the structures labelled **X** and **Y**.

X: ....

Y: ....

(2)

(b) (i) Where in the kidney does the selective reabsorption of glucose take place?

☐ **A** loop of Henle

☐ **B** proximal convoluted tubule

☐ **C** collecting duct

☐ **D** Bowman's capsule

(1)

(ii) Describe the process of ultrafiltration.

....

....

....

....

....

(3)

(Total for Question 6 = 6 marks)

7 As part of a larger research project into the biodiversity of an area, an investigation was carried out into the abundance and distribution of earthworms around a dried up reservoir.

The diagram shows the study area as seen from above.

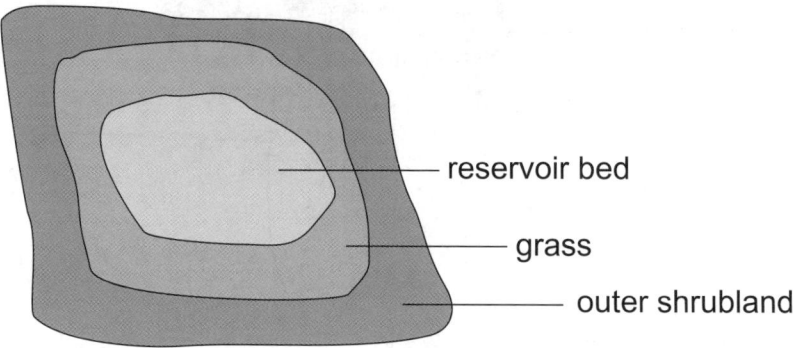

reservoir bed

grass

outer shrubland

(a) State what is meant by the term 'biodiversity'.

....

....

(1)

The scientists began their investigation by estimating the abundance of earthworms in the reservoir bed.

1. They randomly placed ten quadrats, each with an area of 0.5 m², in the bed.

2. At each quadrat, they dug down to a depth of 0.3 m and collected the soil they removed.

3. They then searched through each soil sample and recorded the number of earthworms they found at each quadrat.

(b) (i) Describe what the scientists should have done next in order to estimate the abundance of earthworms in the reservoir bed.

....

....

....

(2)

(ii) Suggest **one** way that the scientists could have got a more accurate estimate of the abundance of earthworms.

....

....

(1)

For the next part of their investigation, the scientists investigated the distribution of earthworms from the centre of the reservoir bed to the outer scrubland.

(c) Describe a method the scientists could have used to produce valid results.

....

....

....

....

....

....

....

....

(4)

The scientists also collected data about the organic material contained in the soil from the centre of the reservoir bed to the outer scrubland.

A summary of their results is shown in the graph below.

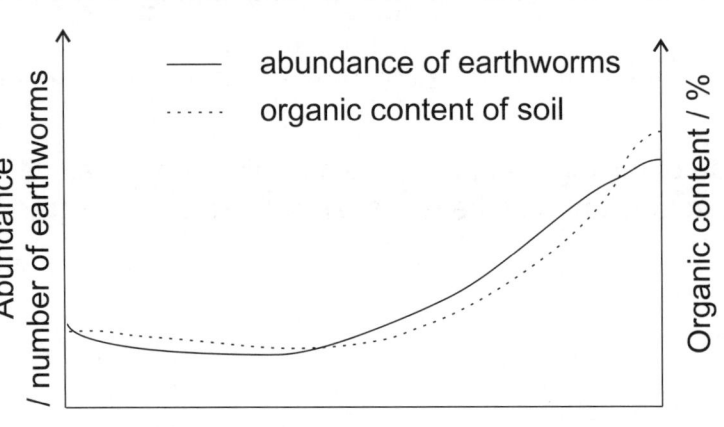

(d) A scientist made the following conclusion based on the results of the investigation:

"Soil containing high levels of organic material leads to a greater abundance of earthworms."

Give **one** reason why this is **not** a valid conclusion.

....

....

(1)

Much of the organic matter found in soil is the remains of dead organisms. Earthworms feed on this organic material.

(e) Explain how the earthworms feeding on organic material in the soil contributes to the carbon cycle.

....

....

....

(2)

(Total for Question 7 = 11 marks)

TOTAL FOR PAPER = 70 MARKS

BEHPI41U

CGP

Edexcel International GCSE

Biology

For the Grade 9-1 Course

Practice Exam Papers
Instructions & Answer Book

Perfect exam practice from CGP!

You can't bluff your way through Edexcel's International GCSE Biology exams.
No chance. What you need is a way of making sure you're 100% prepared.

That's where this brilliant pack from CGP comes in. It contains two full sets of realistic
mock exams, so you get used to tackling the types of questions examiners love to ask
— all in the comfort of your own home / classroom / private jet.

We've also included full answers and mark schemes for each paper, so it's easy to check how
you're getting on. You'll be ready for anything when the real exams roll around.

What to Expect in The Exams

① *There will be Two Papers*

For Edexcel International
GCSE Biology, you'll sit
<u>two exam papers</u> at the
<u>end</u> of your course.

Paper	Time	No. of marks
1	2 hours	110
2	1 hr 15 mins	70

*Some of the course
content will only be
assessed in Paper 2.*

② *You'll be Tested on your Maths...*

Some of the marks for Edexcel International GCSE Biology come from questions on the
<u>maths skills</u> you've used in the course. You'll be expected to handle data in the exam,
so make sure you know how to do things like find the <u>mean</u>, <u>median</u> and <u>mode</u>.

③ *...and on your Practical Skills*

- Edexcel International GCSE Biology contains <u>fourteen practical investigations</u> that
  you'll do during the course — but you can also be asked about them in the exams.

- For example, you might be asked to comment on the <u>design</u> of an experiment
  (the <u>apparatus</u> and <u>methods</u>), make <u>predictions</u>, <u>analyse</u> or <u>interpret results</u>...
  Pretty much anything to do with planning and carrying out the investigations.

*You could be asked about
practical investigations
you're unfamiliar with too.
So you'll need to be able to
apply the skills you've learnt
to other experiments.*

Marking Your Papers

- Do a complete exam set (Paper 1 and Paper 2).

- Use the answers and mark scheme in this booklet to mark each exam paper.

- Write down your mark for each paper in the table below —
  Paper 1 is worth 110 marks and Paper 2 is worth 70 marks.

- Find your total for the whole exam (out of a maximum of 180 marks)
  by adding up your marks from both papers.

- Follow the instructions below to estimate your grade.

	Paper 1	Paper 2	Total mark	Grade
SET A				
SET B				

Estimating Your Grade

- If you want to get a **rough idea** of the grade you're working at, we suggest you compare the **total mark** you got in **each set** to the latest set of grade boundaries.

- Grade boundaries are set for each individual exam, so they're likely to **change** from year to year. You can find the latest set of grade boundaries by going to
  www.cgpbooks.co.uk/gcsegradeboundaries

- Jot down the marks required for each grade in the table below so you don't have to refer back to the website. Use these marks to **estimate your grade**.
  If you're borderline, don't push yourself up a grade — the real examiners won't.

Total mark required for each grade									
Grade	9	8	7	6	5	4	3	2	1
Total mark out of 180									

- Remember, this will only be a **rough guide**, and grade boundaries will be different for different exams, but it should help you to see how you're getting on.

Published by CGP

Editors: Ellen Burton, Mary Falkner, Hayley Thompson.
Contributor: Alison Popperwell.
Proofreaders: Philip Armstrong, Katie Fernandez.

Many thanks to Jan Greenway for the copyright research.

Clipart from Corel®
Illustrations by: Sandy Gardner Artist, email
sandy@sandygardner.co.uk
Printed by Zenith Print & Packaging Ltd, Pontypridd.

Text, design, layout and original illustrations
© Coordination Group Publications Ltd. (CGP) 2020
All rights reserved.

Answers

1 a) A *[1 mark]*

   b) i)

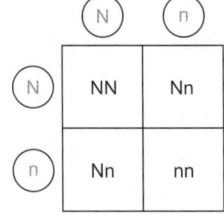

[1 mark]

   ii) Proportion of offspring expected to have vestigial wings
       = 25%/0.25/1 in 4
       So out of 200 fruit flies, the expected number of
       offspring with vestigial wings = (200 ÷ 100) × 25 / 200
       × 0.25 / 200 ÷ 4 = **50**
       [2 marks for the correct answer, otherwise 1 mark for the
       correct proportion of offspring expected to have vestigial
       wings.]

Remember, the allele for vestigial wings is recessive, so only offspring
with the genotype 'nn' will have vestigial wings.

   c) Genetic material is stored as DNA molecules *[1 mark]*,
       which are arranged into chromosomes *[1 mark]*. The
       chromosomes are found in the nucleus of each cell
       [1 mark].

2 a) To make sure the results were representative of the
       whole population in each section. / To prevent bias.
       [1 mark]

   b) i) 52 *[1 mark]*

Remember, the median is the middle value of a data set when the
data is in numerical order.

   ii) Mean number of clover per m^2 = (87 + 96 + 88) ÷ 3
       = 90.333... = **90** (2 s.f.)
       [2 marks for the correct answer, otherwise 1 mark for
       90.333...]

   iii) area of section C = 5 × 3 = 15 m^2
        12 × 15 = **180 dandelions**
        [2 marks for correct answer, otherwise 1 mark for correct
        working]

   c) E.g. all three species were more common in section B
       than section A / the population size of all three species
       was higher in section B than section A / all three species
       were found more frequently in section B than section A
       [1 mark].

   d) Any three from: e.g. differences in temperature /
       differences in the mineral content of the soil / differences
       in the soil pH / differences in the light intensity received
       by the plants / differences in the moisture level of the
       soil / differences in the wind intensity/direction *[3 marks*
       — 1 mark for each correct answer]

Remember, abiotic factors are non-living parts of an ecosystem.

3 a) A *[1 mark]*

   b) i) Any two from: e.g. plasmids *[1 mark]* / single loop of
          DNA *[1 mark]* / no nucleus *[1 mark]*.

   ii) E.g. some white blood cells (phagocytes) will carry out
       phagocytosis *[1 mark]*— this involves engulfing the
       bacteria and digesting them *[1 mark]*. / Some types of
       white blood cell (lymphocytes) will release antibodies
       [1 mark]. These will be specific to the *Salmonella*
       bacteria, locking on to its antigens and causing the
       bacteria to be targeted for destruction by other white
       blood cells *[1 mark]*.

   c) i) Any two from: e.g. a protein coat *[1 mark]*. /
          One type of nucleic acid (RNA or DNA) *[1 mark]*. /
          No nucleus/subcellular structures *[1 mark]*.

   ii) E.g. it prevents the formation of chloroplasts *[1 mark]*,
       resulting in the discolouring of the leaves / reducing the
       rate of photosynthesis/growth *[1 mark]*.

4 a) i) Stage: B *[1 mark]*. Reason: e.g. this stage results in the
         division of a single cell into identical cells/clones, each
         of which has a full copy of the genetic material *[1 mark]*.

   ii) growth / repair *[1 mark]*

   b) D *[1 mark]*

5 a) i) E.g. they don't shed much hair *[1 mark]*.

   ii) Initially Labrador retrievers with a gentle temperament
       could be bred with poodles that don't shed much hair/
       don't cause a reaction in people with dog allergies
       [1 mark]. From the offspring, dogs with the most gentle
       temperaments and that shed the least hair/cause the
       least reaction in people with dog allergies could be bred
       together *[1 mark]*. This process could be repeated over
       many generations until dogs with a gentle temperament
       and that don't shed much hair/are suitable for people
       with dog allergies are consistently created *[1 mark]*.

   b) i) B *[1 mark]*

   ii) E.g. the farmer could have applied a fertiliser *[1 mark]*,
       which would provide more of the minerals the wheat
       needs to grow *[1 mark]*. / The farmer could have applied
       a pesticide *[1 mark]*, which would reduce the amount of
       wheat being damaged or destroyed by pests *[1 mark]*.

6 a) Similarity: both producers use energy from non-living
       sources to increase their biomass/provide food for other
       organisms in a food web *[1 mark]*.
       Difference: the bacteria use chemicals in the deep sea
       vent to do this, whereas plants use energy from the Sun
       [1 mark].

   b) D *[1 mark]*

   c) Any three from: e.g. some parts of the shrimp will not
       be eaten by the fish *[1 mark]*. / Some parts of the shrimp
       will be indigestible *[1 mark]*. / The fish will use some of
       the energy they take in for life processes, like respiration
       and movement *[1 mark]*. / Some of the energy that the
       fish take in is transferred to the surroundings by heat
       [1 mark].

d) Any four from: e.g. the population of crabs might decrease in size, as there would be fewer tubeworms for them to eat *[1 mark]*. / Fewer crabs could cause the population of octopuses to decrease in size as they would have less food to eat *[1 mark]*. / The population of bacteria might increase as there would be fewer tubeworms to eat them *[1 mark]*. / If the population of bacteria increases, the population size of the shrimps might rise, as there would be more bacteria for them to eat *[1 mark]*. / More shrimps might lead to an increase in the population size of fish, as they would have more food to eat *[1 mark]*. / More fish could lead to a rise in the population size of octopuses as they would also have more food to eat *[1 mark]*.

e)

```
        ┌┐
        ││ Octopuses
      ┌──┴┴──┐
      │ Fish │ ◄─ (Bar 1.2 cm wide)
   ┌──┴──────┴──┐
   │   Shrimp   │
   └────────────┘
```

[1 mark]

7 Any six from: e.g. the palisade mesophyll cells contain a large number of chloroplasts for photosynthesis *[1 mark]*. / The palisade mesophyll cells are close to the surface of the leaf, where they can get the most light *[1 mark]*. / The upper epidermis is transparent, which allows light to pass through this tissue to the palisade mesophyll layer below *[1 mark]*. / The lower epidermis contains pores called stomata, which allow carbon dioxide to diffuse directly into the leaf tissue *[1 mark]*. / There is a waxy cuticle to reduce water loss by evaporation *[1 mark]*. / The vascular bundles contain xylem vessels, which transport water to the leaf *[1 mark]*. / The spongy mesophyll contains air spaces, which increase the surface area for gas exchange *[1 mark]*.

8 a) i) amylase *[1 mark]* and maltase *[1 mark]*
   ii) E.g. add iodine solution to the sample *[1 mark]*. If the iodine solution remains browny-orange then the starch has been broken down. / If the iodine solution turns black/blue-black then the starch has not been broken down *[1 mark]*.

b) i) A *[1 mark]*
   ii) Bile emulsifies fat/breaks fat down into tiny droplets *[1 mark]*. This gives a large surface area for enzymes/ lipases to work on *[1 mark]*. By blocking the bile ducts, the gallstones could prevent bile from entering the small intestine *[1 mark]*. Without bile, any fats would be digested more slowly *[1 mark]*.

c) i) X = (19.0 × 3) − 19.5 − 17.5 = **20.0 cm³** *[1 mark]*
   All of the data in the question is given to one decimal place, so your answer should also be given to one decimal place.
   ii) A *[1 mark]*

9 a) Oxygen moves into cells by diffusion *[1 mark]*. There's a net movement of oxygen from a higher concentration outside the cell to a lower concentration of oxygen inside the cell *[1 mark]* through the partially permeable cell membrane *[1 mark]*.

b) The rate of oxygen movement across the cell membrane will increase *[1 mark]*. This is because the cell will be using more oxygen (due to the increased rate of aerobic respiration) *[1 mark]*. This will make the concentration gradient of oxygen across the cell membrane steeper/ increase the difference in the concentration of oxygen between the inside and outside of the cell *[1 mark]*.

c) As single-celled organisms, *Euglena* have a large surface area to volume ratio *[1 mark]*. This means they can absorb enough oxygen to survive by diffusion through their outer surface *[1 mark]*. However, as multicellular organisms, trout have a small surface area to volume ratio *[1 mark]*. Diffusion of oxygen across their outer surface would be too slow to supply all their needs, so trout need specialised exchange organs in order to absorb enough oxygen to survive *[1 mark]*.

d) Any five from: e.g. set up a water bath to get the components of the experiment to a certain temperature *[1 mark]*. / Add a mixture of sugar, yeast and distilled water to a test tube *[1 mark]*. / Add a layer of oil to the top of the mixture to create anaerobic conditions *[1 mark]*. / Attach a bung to the test tube with a tube leading to a test tube of water *[1 mark]*. / Count how many bubbles of CO_2 are produced in one minute. / Repeat the experiment at different temperatures *[1 mark]*. / Control the other variables, such as the concentration of sugar, each time the repeat is carried out *[1 mark]*.

10 a)

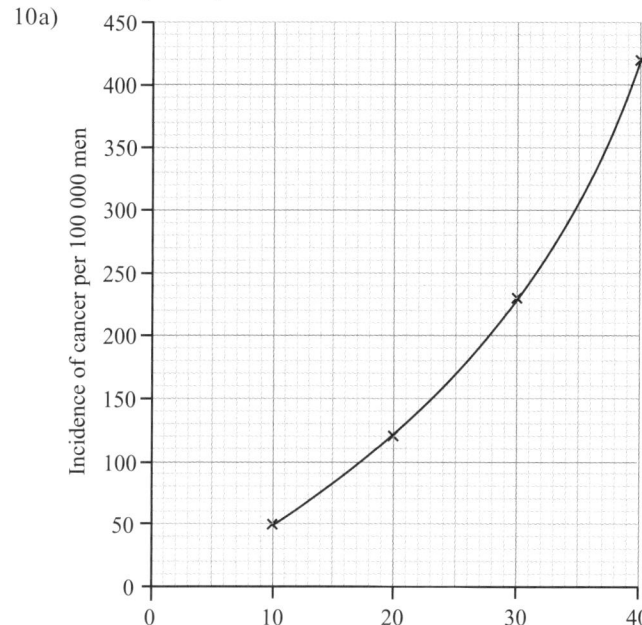

[4 marks — 1 mark for a label and suitable scale for the x-axis, 1 mark for a label and suitable scale for the y-axis, 1 mark for plotting all data points correctly, 1 mark for drawing a smooth curve of best fit.]

When you're drawing a curve or line of best fit on a graph, you shouldn't extend it past the plotted points. That's why the curve on this graph hasn't been extended to the origin (the point where the axes meet).

b) No. E.g. the data shows the incidence of cancer, not deaths from cancer *[1 mark]*. The data also only shows the incidence of cancer in men not women, so you can't say this trend is true for everyone *[1 mark]*. Finally the data is only given for smokers, so you can't compare the likelihood of developing cancer in smokers and non-smokers *[1 mark]*.

11a) E.g. carbon dioxide is released into the atmosphere when humans burn fossil fuels *[1 mark]*. Cattle-rearing/rice growing produces methane gas *[1 mark]*. Nitrous oxide is released from fertilisers/vehicle engines *[1 mark]*. CFCs can be released from leaks from old fridges *[1 mark]*. By increasing the amount of these greenhouse gases in the atmosphere, human activity is enhancing the greenhouse effect *[1 mark]*. This means more heat is being radiated back to the Earth, warming it up *[1 mark]*.

You could have named any valid examples of human activities that contribute to global warming.

b) C *[1 mark]*

12a) i) E.g.

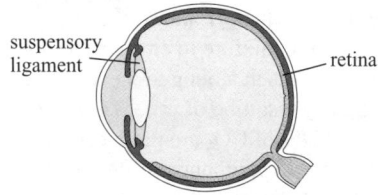

suspensory ligament   retina

[2 marks — 1 for each correct label]

ii) The iris contains muscles *[1 mark]*, which allow it to control the diameter of the pupil and therefore the amount of light entering the eye *[1 mark]*.

iii) The ciliary muscles relax *[1 mark]*, which allows the suspensory ligaments to pull tight *[1 mark]*. This makes the lens go thin *[1 mark]*, so it refracts light by a smaller amount *[1 mark]*.

b) i) Hormone: adrenaline *[1 mark]*
Source: adrenal glands *[1 mark]*
Effect: e.g. the heart muscle contracts more frequently and with more force *[1 mark]*, so oxygen supply to the tissues/blood flow to the muscles increases *[1 mark]*.

ii) E.g. sweat will be produced *[1 mark]*. When this evaporates, energy is transferred from the skin to the environment *[1 mark]*. Vasodilation will occur/the blood vessels close to the surface of the skin will widen *[1 mark]*. This allows more blood to flow near the surface, so more energy is transferred to the surroundings *[1 mark]*.

Set A — Paper 2

1 a) asexual reproduction *[1 mark]*

b) D *[1 mark]*

c) Advantage: e.g. using pesticides means that fewer plants will be damaged, increasing the yield of strawberries *[1 mark]*.
Disadvantages: e.g. pesticides are often poisonous to humans, so they must be used carefully to keep the amount of pesticide in the fruit below a safe level *[1 mark]*. Pesticides can harm wildlife *[1 mark]*.

d) Using another living organism to reduce pest numbers *[1 mark]*.

e) Strawberry plants are pollinated by insects *[1 mark]*.

f) At pollination, a pollen grain lands on the stigma of a flower *[1 mark]*. A pollen tube grows out of the pollen grain and down through the style to the ovary and into the ovule *[1 mark]*. A nucleus from the male gamete moves down the tube and fertilises a female gamete in the ovule *[1 mark]*. The fertilised female gamete develops into a seed *[1 mark]*.

g) Any two from: e.g. as the plants are enclosed, it's easier to keep them free of pests/disease *[1 mark]*. / Keeping the plants enclosed makes it easier for farmers to control the water supplied to them *[1 mark]*. / Plants can be easily supplied with artificial light to give them more time to photosynthesise *[1 mark]*. / It's easier to keep the plants at an ideal temperature for photosynthesis, since the structures trap the Sun's heat/can be heated *[1 mark]*. / The level of carbon dioxide inside can be kept high (e.g. with a paraffin heater), increasing the rate of photosynthesis *[1 mark]*.

2 a) Males have one X chromosome and one Y chromosome *[1 mark]*. Females have two X chromosomes *[1 mark]*.

b) C *[1 mark]*

c) The new cell divides by mitosis *[1 mark]*. The two new cells continue to divide to create lots of new cells in the embryo *[1 mark]*. As the embryo develops, the cells differentiate into the specialised cells that make the organism *[1 mark]*.

d) The mRNA molecule moves out of the nucleus into the cytoplasm *[1 mark]* and joins up with a ribosome *[1 mark]*. Amino acids are brought to the ribosome by tRNA *[1 mark]*. Each tRNA molecule contains an anticodon, which is complementary to the codon for an amino acid *[1 mark]*. The anticodon on the tRNA pairs up with a codon on the mRNA, so that amino acids are brought to the ribosome in the correct order *[1 mark]*. The amino acids are joined together by the ribosome to form a protein *[1 mark]*.

3 a) B *[1 mark]*

b) platelets *[1 mark]*

c) i) Having more red blood cells means that more oxygen can be carried to the muscles *[1 mark]*. This may improve an athlete's performance during a race as it means there is more oxygen available for aerobic respiration *[1 mark]*. This means more energy can be transferred for muscle contraction *[1 mark]*, allowing the athlete to run faster/run for longer *[1 mark]*.

ii) E.g. red blood cells have a biconcave shape *[1 mark]*. This gives them a large surface area for absorbing and releasing oxygen *[1 mark]*. / Red blood cells contain lots of haemoglobin *[1 mark]*. Haemoglobin binds to oxygen, allowing it to be transported, so this means red blood cells can pick up lots of oxygen in the lungs and then release it in body tissues *[1 mark]*. / Red blood cells don't have a nucleus *[1 mark]*. This frees up space for more haemoglobin, so they can carry more oxygen *[1 mark]*.

d) Blood vessel A: artery
Reason: it has thick walls / thick layers of muscle and elastic in its walls / a small lumen relative to the thickness of its walls. *[1 mark for 'artery' plus correct reason.]*
Blood vessel B: vein
Reason: it has thin walls / thin layers of muscle and elastic in its walls / a large lumen relative to the thickness of its walls. *[1 mark for 'vein' plus correct reason.]*

4 a) It will increase *[1 mark]* because water molecules will move from the area of higher water concentration in the beaker *[1 mark]* to the area of lower water concentration inside the Visking tubing *[1 mark]*.

b) E.g. set up the same apparatus with different concentrations of sugar solution inside the Visking tubing *[1 mark]*. Leave the apparatus for a set amount of time/30 minutes *[1 mark]*. Compare the change in volume inside the capillary tube for each solution to determine how the concentration of the sugar solution affected the rate of osmosis *[1 mark]*.

c) i) mean change in mass = $(-1.2 + -1.5 + -1.2) \div 3$
$= -3.9 \div 3 = $ **−1.3 g** *[1 mark]*

ii) change in mass = $6.2 - 5.1 = -1.1$ g
percentage change = $(-1.1 \div 6.2) \times 100$
$= -17.74... = $ **−18%** (to 2 s.f.)
[2 marks for correct answer given to 2 significant figures, otherwise 1 mark for finding the change in mass.]

5 a) Point at which ADH is most likely to be released: B *[1 mark]*. Explanation: this is where the water content of the blood is lowest *[1 mark]*. ADH is released when the water content of the blood is too low, so the kidneys reabsorb more water/to increase the water content of the blood *[1 mark]*.

b) i) pituitary gland *[1 mark]*
ii) It will cause more concentrated urine to be produced *[1 mark]*.

6 a) The nucleus was removed from an unfertilised sheep's egg cell *[1 mark]*. A nucleus taken from an adult body cell of another sheep was then inserted into the egg cell *[1 mark]*. The egg cell was then stimulated to divide to form an embryo by being given an electric shock *[1 mark]*. The embryo was then implanted into the womb of an adult female sheep *[1 mark]*, where it developed into Dolly, a clone of the adult that the body cell came from *[1 mark]*.

b) E.g. nutrients *[1 mark]* and growth hormones *[1 mark]*.

7 a) E.g. the paper on the lower surface of the leaf got wet, whereas the paper on the upper surface of the leaf did not *[1 mark]*. This is because more water escaped from the lower surface of the leaf *[1 mark]*, suggesting that there are more stomata on this surface / bigger stomata on this surface *[1 mark]*.

b) E.g. because the experimental conditions / the humidity/temperature/air movement/light intensity may be different on different days *[1 mark]* which would affect the transpiration rate of the plant, changing the results *[1 mark]*.

c) i) 12.00 hours *[1 mark]*. This is when the rate of water uptake, and therefore the rate of transpiration, is greatest *[1 mark]* so the stomata are most likely to be fully open *[1 mark]*.

ii) E.g. the light intensity/temperature is likely to have increased between 00.00 and 12.00 *[1 mark]*. This will have increased the transpiration rate of the plant and therefore its rate of water uptake, as shown in the graph *[1 mark]*. Between 12.00 and 24.00, the light intensity/temperature is likely to have decreased *[1 mark]*, leading to a corresponding decrease in the rate of water uptake *[1 mark]*.

iii) Change in mass of plant (g)
= rate of water uptake (g/hour) × time (hours)
= $1.5 \times 3 = $ **4.5 g**
[2 marks for correct answer, otherwise 1 mark for correctly rearranging the formula.]

Set B — Paper 1

1 a)   C *[1 mark]*
  b) i) E.g. the number of puffins might decrease *[1 mark]* because there would be fewer herring for them to eat *[1 mark]*.
    ii) E.g. the number of zooplankton might increase *[1 mark]* because there would be fewer herring to eat them *[1 mark]*.

2 a)   spinal cord *[1 mark]*
  b)   D *[1 mark]*
  c)   Any four from: e.g. receptors in the fingers detect a stimulus *[1 mark]*. / Nervous impulses travel from receptors along a sensory neurone to the spinal cord *[1 mark]*. / In the spinal cord, nervous impulses are passed to a relay neurone *[1 mark]*. / Impulses travel from the spinal cord along a motor neurone to the arm muscle/effector, which then contracts *[1 mark]*. / When a synapse is reached, the nervous impulse is transmitted between neurones by a neurotransmitter that diffuses across the gap *[1 mark]*.

3 a)   A *[1 mark]*
  b)   E.g. some of the bacteria developed random mutations in their DNA that meant they were less affected by isoniazid and rifampicin *[1 mark]*. In patients being treated for tuberculosis, bacteria with these mutations were more likely to survive the antibiotics *[1 mark]*, so these bacteria would live longer and reproduce many more times *[1 mark]*. This led to the alleles for resistance being passed on to lots of offspring, so they became more common in the population over time/resistant strains of the bacteria developed. *[1 mark]*.

4 a)   E.g. because the cotton wool allows air/oxygen to enter the flasks / carbon dioxide to escape *[1 mark]*.
  b) i) Flask A shows an overall increase in temperature over the 5 days *[1 mark]*.
    ii) The beans in Flask A were respiring *[1 mark]* and respiration transfers energy to the surroundings, which would have increased the temperature in the flask *[1 mark]*.
  c)   The boiled beans would have been dead / their enzymes would have been denatured *[1 mark]* and therefore the beans would not have respired *[1 mark]*. This allowed them to act as a control for the experiment *[1 mark]*.

5 a) i) A and C *[1 mark]*
    ii) Breed the two varieties of plants together to combine the desired characteristics *[1 mark]*. Select plants from the offspring that show most of the desired characteristics and breed them together *[1 mark]*. Repeat this process over several generations until you get raspberry plants with all the desired characteristics *[1 mark]*.
  b) i) E.g. a section of DNA that codes for a characteristic that could increase food production, e.g. a gene for insect resistance, is identified *[1 mark]*. This DNA is cut out with a restriction enzyme *[1 mark]*. A plasmid or a virus can be used as a vector to transfer DNA into a cell *[1 mark]*. This vector DNA is cut open using the same restriction enzyme that was used to cut out the desired DNA section *[1 mark]*. Ligase enzymes are used to join the two pieces of DNA together *[1 mark]*. This recombinant DNA can then be inserted into the cells of the plant that is being modified *[1 mark]*.
    ii) E.g. large quantities of human insulin can be made *[1 mark]* from genetically modified bacteria grown in a fermenter *[1 mark]*.

6 a)   B *[1 mark]*
  b)   Any two from: e.g. they have a good blood supply *[1 mark]*, which maintains the concentration gradient of gases for diffusion *[1 mark]*. / They have thin/permeable walls *[1 mark]*, so gases only have a short distance to diffuse *[1 mark]*. / They have a large surface area *[1 mark]*, so lots of gas molecules can diffuse at once *[1 mark]*.
  c) i) trachea, bronchus, bronchiole, alveolus *[1 mark]*
    ii) B *[1 mark]*
  d)   E.g. a volunteer should sit still for five minutes. The number of breaths they take in the minute following this rest period should be counted (this is their resting breathing rate). All time periods should be measured with a stopwatch. The volunteer should then cycle on an exercise bike at the slowest speed setting for five minutes. The number of breaths they take in the minute immediately following this period of exercise should be counted and recorded. The person should be given enough time to return to their resting breathing rate, before repeating the test twice more. The whole experiment should then be repeated at a series of higher speed settings and the mean result for each speed setting compared. Each time a repeat is carried out, the same person should exercise for the same amount of time, in a room of the same temperature.
[1 mark for including a control (i.e. recording the breathing rate at rest), 1 mark for describing how the breathing rate should be measured, 1 mark for varying the speed setting on the bike, 1 mark for stating that the investigation should be repeated at each speed setting, 1 mark for controlling one variable (e.g. the length of the exercise period / temperature at which the experiment takes place / same person doing the exercise), 1 mark for controlling a second variable. Maximum 5 marks available.]

It's important that the same person does the cycling at each speed, since different people's breathing rates will be differently affected by exercise, e.g. because of their level of fitness. You could repeat the whole experiment using different volunteers though, to see whether the results always follow the same pattern.

7 a)   X: surface area of one side = $0.5 \times 0.5 = 0.25$
surface area of cube = $0.25 \times 6 =$ **1.5 mm²** *[1 mark]*
Y: $0.1 \times 0.1 \times 0.1 =$ **0.001 mm³** *[1 mark]*
Z: $0.54 \div 0.027 =$ **20 : 1** *[1 mark]*
  b) $60 \div 12 =$ **5** times bigger *[1 mark]*
  c)   Cube: A *[1 mark]*
Explanation: Cube A has the smallest surface area to volume ratio so the rate of exchange across its surface would be the slowest *[1 mark]*.
  d)   E.g. warmer water would increase the rate of exchange *[1 mark]* because the diffusing particles would have more energy and therefore move around more *[1 mark]*.
  e) i) E.g. amoeba *[1 mark]*
    ii) E.g. fungi / yeast *[1 mark]*

8 a) i) Name: placenta *[1 mark]*
        Function: allows food, oxygen and waste to be exchanged
        between the blood of the fetus and the mother *[1 mark]*.
   ii) amniotic fluid *[1 mark]*
   b) E.g.

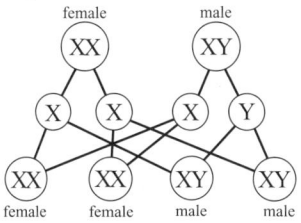

*[1 mark for males having the chromosomes XY and females
having the chromosomes XX. 1 mark for a correct genetic
cross producing a 50 : 50 ratio.]*
*You could have drawn a Punnett square here instead and still got the
marks if the chromosomes and cross were shown correctly.*
   c) i) Any two from: e.g. extra hair on face and body /
        development of muscles / enlargement of penis and
        testicles / sperm production / deepening of voice
        [1 mark for two].
   ii) plasma *[1 mark]*
9 a) 6O₂ *[1 mark]*
   b) A *[1 mark]*
*Between points A and B on the graph, the rate of photosynthesis
increases as light intensity increases, so light intensity is the limiting
factor (stopping photosynthesis happening any faster). After point B,
increasing the light intensity does not alter the rate of photosynthesis
(the graph levels off) so it is no longer the limiting factor.*
   c) At this light intensity, the rate of photosynthesis is
       higher at 0.4% carbon dioxide than at 0.04% carbon
       dioxide *[1 mark]*. The temperature is the same at
       both concentrations, suggesting that a carbon dioxide
       concentration of 0.04% is the limiting factor *[1 mark]*.
   d) i)

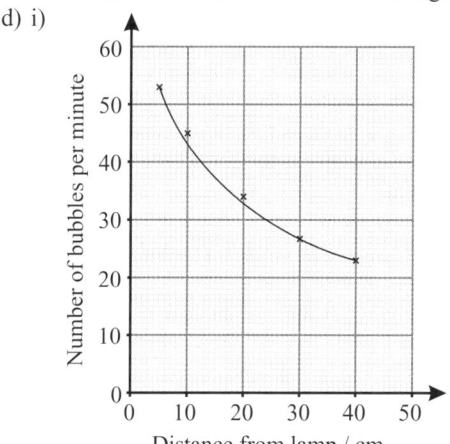

*[4 marks — 1 mark for a label and suitable scale for
the x-axis, 1 mark for a label and suitable scale for
the y-axis, 1 mark for correctly plotted points and
1 mark for a correctly drawn curve of best fit.]*
   ii) 21 cm (allow any answer between 20 and 22 cm) *[1 mark]*
*To find the answer, rule directly across from 32 on the y-axis to the curve
of best fit. Then rule directly down from the curve to the x-axis and read
off the value.*
   iii) E.g. increasing the light intensity increases the rate of
        photosynthesis in pondweed *[1 mark]*. At lower light
        intensities, changing the light intensity has a smaller effect
        on the rate of photosynthesis than it does at higher light
        intensities *[1 mark]*.

10   E.g. the pulmonary vein brings oxygenated blood from
     the lungs into the left atrium *[1 mark]*. The left atrium
     contracts, pushing the blood through a valve into the
     left ventricle *[1 mark]*. The left ventricle then contracts,
     pushing the blood out of the heart through a valve into the
     aorta *[1 mark]*. The blood then travels around the body,
     before re-entering the right atrium through the vena cava
     [1 mark]. The right atrium then contracts, pushing the
     blood through a valve into the right ventricle *[1 mark]*. The
     right ventricle then contracts and pushes the deoxygenated
     blood through a valve into the pulmonary artery towards
     the lungs *[1 mark]*.
11a) glycerol and fatty acids *[1 mark]*
   b) Aerobic respiration takes place in the presence of oxygen,
       while anaerobic respiration takes place in the absence of
       oxygen *[1 mark]*. The products of aerobic respiration in
       animals are carbon dioxide and water, while the product
       of anaerobic respiration in animals is lactic acid *[1 mark]*.
       Aerobic respiration transfers more energy/produces more
       ATP than anaerobic respiration *[1 mark]*.
   c) i) Add biuret solution to the sample of dog food *[1 mark]*.
        If the sample turns from blue to purple, then the food
        contains proteins *[1 mark]*.
   ii) Any four from: e.g. bile is likely to be released from the
        dog's gall bladder into its small intestine *[1 mark]*. / Bile
        will emulsify the fats/break the fats into tiny droplets to
        give a bigger surface area (for lipase digestion) *[1 mark]*. /
        Bile creates an optimum/alkaline pH for enzymes/lipases in
        the small intestine to function *[1 mark]*. / Lipases are likely
        to be produced by the dog's pancreas and small intestine
        [1 mark]. / Lipases break down lipid droplets into smaller
        molecules (glycerol and fatty acids) *[1 mark]*.
12a) The chromosome number is halved during meiosis (when
      the gametes are formed) *[1 mark]*. In the diagram, this is
      shown by cells with the genotype 'Rr' producing gametes
      with the genotypes 'R' and 'r' *[1 mark]*. The chromosome
      number is restored at fertilisation when the gametes fuse
      [1 mark]. This is shown in the diagram by gametes with
      the genotypes 'R' and 'r' producing offspring with the
      genotypes 'RR', 'Rr' and 'rr' *[1 mark]*.
   b) 3 : 1 *[1 mark]*
   c) E.g.

	father's gametes	
	r	r
R	Rr	Rr
r	rr	rr

mother's
gametes

0.5 / 1/2 / 50% of offspring are expected to have smooth
hair.
Number of offspring in litter = 6
Expected number of offspring with smooth hair = 6 ÷ 2 = **3**
*[5 marks — 1 mark for correctly identifying the mother's/
female guinea pig's gametes as Rr, 1 mark for correctly
identifying the father's/male guinea pig's gametes as
rr, 1 mark for correctly identifying the genotypes of the
offspring as Rr, Rr, rr and rr, 2 marks for the expected
number of offspring with smooth hair = 3, otherwise
1 mark for correctly calculating the probability of offspring
inheriting smooth hair as 0.5 / 1/2 / 50%.]*
   d) Hair type in guinea pigs is the result of a single gene,
       whereas most phenotypic characteristics are the result of
       polygenic inheritance/several genes interacting *[1 mark]*.

13 a) Because active transport is a process which requires energy *[1 mark]* and mitochondria provide energy for a cell through aerobic respiration *[1 mark]*.

b) E.g. algae may have competed with the seedlings for the mineral/nitrate ions in the solutions *[1 mark]*, which could have affected the seedlings' growth *[1 mark]*.

c) Difference: e.g. the seedling in tube A would be smaller/ shorter than the seedling in tube B *[1 mark]*.
Explanation: e.g. tube A was lacking in nitrates *[1 mark]* which are needed (to make proteins) for the plant's growth *[1 mark]*.

d) E.g. the solution used in the experiment did not contain enough magnesium ions for the seedlings / the seedlings had used up the magnesium ions in the solutions by this point *[1 mark]*.

Set B — Paper 2

1 a) A specialised cell is a cell whose structure allows it to carry out a particular function *[1 mark]*.

b) zygote *[1 mark]*

A zygote is produced by the fusion of a male and female gamete at fertilisation. It then divides to form an embryo, the first cells of which are stem cells.

c) i) E.g. the cornea refracts (bends) light into the eye *[1 mark]* so that it can be focussed onto the retina by the lens *[1 mark]*. If the cornea is damaged, it may not be able to refract the light correctly, so light may not reach the retina/ less light may reach the retina, causing sight loss/reducing a person's ability to see clearly *[1 mark]*.

ii) E.g. the stem cells could be made to divide and differentiate *[1 mark]* into specialised cornea cells *[1 mark]*, which could be transplanted into the cornea and used to replace the damaged cells *[1 mark]*.

d) i) E.g. sensory neurones carry nervous impulses from sensory receptors to the CNS *[1 mark]*. Damage to sensory neurones could cause loss of sensation as the brain wouldn't receive information about stimuli from the receptors *[1 mark]*. Motor neurones carry nervous impulses from the CNS to effectors such as muscles *[1 mark]*. If a motor neurone is damaged, the brain won't be able to instruct the muscle it connects with to contract, so the muscle will be paralysed *[1 mark]*.

ii) Advantage: e.g. embryonic stem cells are more versatile than adult stem cells and can turn into any cell type in the body *[1 mark]*. / It may be harder/riskier to obtain stem cells from an adult body *[1 mark]*. Disadvantage: e.g. there are ethical concerns surrounding the use of embryonic stem cells as it involves the destruction of embryos *[1 mark]*.

2 a) B *[1 mark]*

b) During daylight hours (when light intensity is high) plants make more oxygen by photosynthesis than they use in respiration *[1 mark]*. They also use up more carbon dioxide than they produce *[1 mark]*, so in daylight, plants release oxygen into the atmosphere and take in carbon dioxide *[1 mark]*. When it gets dark, plants stop photosynthesising because the light intensity is too low *[1 mark]*. However, they must continue to respire in order to obtain the energy they need to live *[1 mark]*. This means they take in oxygen and release carbon dioxide at night *[1 mark]*.

3 a) C *[1 mark]*

b) i) The fish are protected from interspecific predation, as other species are unable to enter the cages to eat the fish *[1 mark]*. The fish are protected from intraspecific predation as the cages allow younger fish to be kept separately from older fish (preventing the older fish from eating the younger fish) *[1 mark]*.

ii) Any one from: e.g. the movement of the fish is limited by the cage *[1 mark]*. This reduces the amount of energy they use swimming, so they have more energy available for growth *[1 mark]*. / The caged fish can be fed a carefully controlled diet of high quality food pellets *[1 mark]*. This diet may provide them with more energy/protein than they would get in the wild, allowing them to grow bigger *[1 mark]*.

c) Sewage contains both nitrates and phosphates *[1 mark]*. These extra nutrients enter the water, causing algae to grow faster and block out the light *[1 mark]*. Plants below are unable to photosynthesise due to the lack of light and so start to die *[1 mark]*. Microorganisms that feed on dead plants have more to eat, so they increase in number and use up oxygen in the water *[1 mark]*. This can cause other organisms that need oxygen, such as fish, to die *[1 mark]*.

4 a) A always pairs with T, so 24% of the bases must be T. So 24% + 24% = 48% of the bases are either A or T. 100 – 48% = 52% of the bases are either C or G. 52% is shared equally between C and G, so percentage of nucleotides that contain base C = 52% ÷ 2 = **26%**. *[3 marks for the correct answer, otherwise 1 mark for 48% of bases = A or T, and 1 mark for 52% of bases = C or G.]*

b) i) methionine, asparagine, tryptophan *[1 mark]*
   ii) Because it changes the order of amino acids in the protein *[1 mark]*.

c) E.g. through exposure to ionising radiation/gamma rays/ X-rays/UV rays. / Through exposure to chemical mutagens/ some chemicals in tobacco. *[2 marks — 1 mark for each correct answer.]*

d) E.g. most mutations have either no effect on an organism's phenotype or a very small effect on an organism's phenotype *[1 mark]*. Mutations that have a significant effect on the phenotype are very rare, and may be beneficial rather than harmful *[1 mark]*.

5 a) The iodine solution would remain browny-orange *[1 mark]* rather than turning blue-black *[1 mark]*.

b) i)

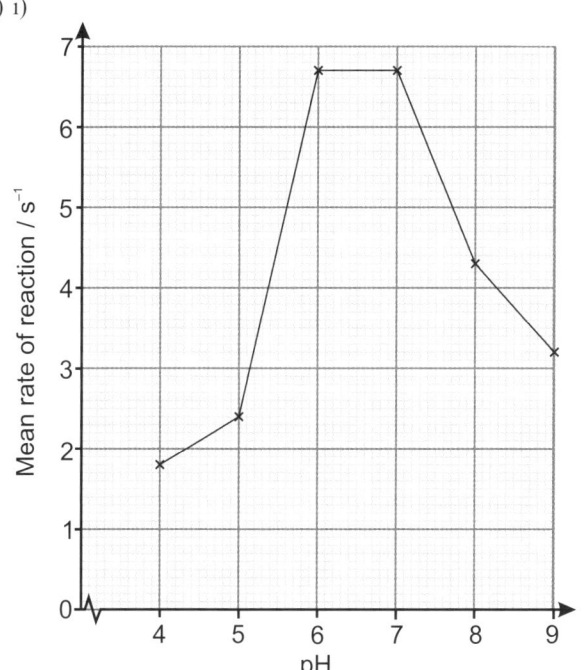

[4 marks — 1 mark for label and suitable scale for x-axis, 2 marks for all 6 points correctly plotted or 1 mark for 5 points correctly plotted, 1 mark for points joined neatly with straight lines.]

ii) Rate of reaction = 4.5 s⁻¹ *[1 mark. Accept any answer between 4.4 and 4.6 s⁻¹.]*

c) E.g. carry out the experiment at pH values between pH 6 and pH 7 *[1 mark]*.

d) E.g. the rate of amylase activity decreases as the pH decreases below pH 6 and as the pH increases above pH 7 *[1 mark]*.

e) E.g. changing the pH interferes with the bonds that hold an enzyme together *[1 mark]*. This changes the shape of the enzyme's active site so that it no longer fits its substrate / denatures the enzyme so that it can no longer function *[1 mark]*.

f) The mouth is connected to one end of the stomach via a muscular tube called the oesophagus *[1 mark]*. The other end of the stomach is connected to the small intestine *[1 mark]*.

6 a) X: ureter *[1 mark]*, Y: urethra *[1 mark]*
   Don't get these the wrong way round. There are two ureters, one from each kidney, but only one urethra.

b) i) B *[1 mark]*
   ii) Blood from the renal artery flows through the capillaries of the glomerulus *[1 mark]*. A high pressure builds up, which squeezes water, urea, ions and glucose out of the blood and into the Bowman's capsule *[1 mark]*. The membranes between the capillaries in the glomerulus and the Bowman's capsule act like filters, so blood cells and large molecules such as proteins are not squeezed out *[1 mark]*.

7 a) Biodiversity is the variety of different species of organisms on Earth or within an ecosystem *[1 mark]*.

b) i) They should have worked out the mean number of organisms per m² *[1 mark]* and then multiplied this number by the total area (in m²) of the reservoir bed *[1 mark]*.
   ii) E.g. they could have used more quadrats. / They could have dug deeper at each quadrat. / They could have used bigger quadrats. *[1 mark]*

c) E.g. the scientists could have used a tape measure to mark out a transect line from the centre of the reservoir bed to the outer scrubland and placed quadrats at regular intervals along it *[1 mark]*. At each quadrat, they could have dug down to a set depth/0.3 m, collected the soil they removed, and counted the number of earthworms they found *[1 mark]*. They could have repeated this process at least three times using transect lines going in different directions from the centre of the reservoir bed *[1 mark]*. Finally they could have calculated the mean number of earthworms found at each distance along the transect lines *[1 mark]*.

d) E.g. there could be factors other than the organic content of the soil affecting the abundance of earthworms *[1 mark]*.

e) The carbon in the organic material is returned to the atmosphere as carbon dioxide *[1 mark]* when the earthworms respire *[1 mark]*.

Acknowledgements

Every effort has been made to locate copyright holders and obtain permission to reproduce sources. For those sources where it has been difficult to trace the originator of the work, we would be grateful for information. If any copyright holder would like us to make an amendment to the acknowledgements, please notify us and we will gladly update the book at the next reprint. Thank you.

CGP